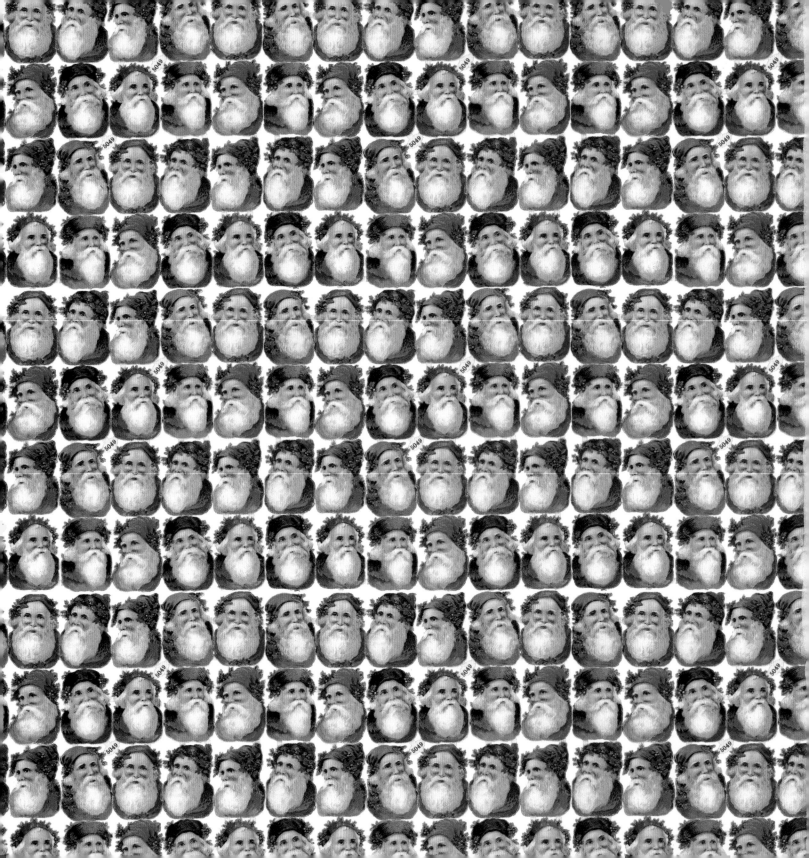

Christmas
2002

For Pat

Wishing you joy all the year long!

Linda Amendt

The Artful Christmas

Holiday Menus & Festive Collectibles

LINDA ARNAUD

PHOTOGRAPHY
MICHEL ARNAUD

DESIGN & ART DIRECTION
JOEL AVIROM

STEWART, TABORI & CHANG
NEW YORK

FOOD STYLING: Jill Raff and Amy Marcus

DESIGN ASSISTANTS: Meghan Day Healey and Jason Snyder

ENDPAPERS: *The jolly faces of Santas are wonderful examples of Victorian "scrap" printed especially for Christmas. During the 1880s it was a popular home activity to collect, cut out and paste beautifully printed images that were made in sheets expressly for scrapbook albums. Homemade ornaments for the tree might also be fashioned from these, mounted on card and decorated with bits of trim.*

Copyright © 2002 by Linda Arnaud

Photographs copyright © 2002 by Michel Arnaud

All rights reserved. No portion of this book may be reproduced, stored in a retrieval system, or transmitted in any form or by any means, mechanical, electronic, photocopying, recording, or otherwise, without written permission from the publisher.

Published in 2002 by Stewart, Tabori & Chang
A Company of La Martinière Groupe
115 West 18th Street
New York, NY 10011

Export Sales to all countries except Canada, France, and French-speaking Switzerland:
Thames and Hudson Ltd.
181A High Holborn
London WC1V 7QX
England

Canadian Distribution:
Canadian Manda Group
One Atlantic Avenue, Suite 105
Toronto, Ontario M6K 3E7
Canada

Library of Congress Cataloging-in-Publication Data
Arnaud, Linda.
    The artful Christmas / by Linda Arnaud.
        p. cm.
    ISBN 1-58479-154-3
        1. Christmas cookery. 2. Menus. I. Title

    TX739.2.C45 A75 2002
    641.5'68—dc21   2002021038

The text of this book was composed in Goudy Village.

Printed in China by C&C Offset

10 9 8 7 6 5 4 3 2 1

First Printing

To the spirit of Christmas—
past, present, and future

E N T S

ACKNOWLEDGMENTS

I AM INDEBTED TO SO MANY PEOPLE WHO GENEROUSLY gave their support and assistance in the making of this book. First among them are Ron and Priscilla Richley who lent their extensive collection of beautiful antique Christmas collectibles to be photographed and shared their expert knowledge of the many traditions of Christmas and its treasures. It was a pleasure to work with them in capturing the joyful spirit of the season on these pages.

My husband Michel Arnaud and my great friend Joel Avirom surpassed themselves in beautifully visualizing eight different Christmas celebrations of my dreams—supported by the diligent work of Jason Snyder, Meghan Day Healey, Liana Fredley, and Jont Enroth.

The assistance of my sister-in-law, Béatrice Arnaud Oliver, in the kitchen and on set during photography was invaluable. Having worked together over the many years to make each Christmas very special for our families, we shared wonderful memories as we worked. And it was a special treat when her twin, Carole Malleville, turned up to give us a hand during a visit from France.

I add grateful thanks to Leslie Stoker and Marisa Bulzone at Stewart, Tabori & Chang for their cheerful support and expert guidance throughout the project.

Private collectors, antique dealers, and shops generously loaned treasured objects, and shared information about the holiday and the collectibles. A special thank you to the dear friends who allowed us to "make Christmas" in their homes—their cheerful patience was greatly appreciated.

Special acknowledgments for their assistance are offered to Sandy and Joe Klempner, Joe Chapman, William Hicks and William Sadler, Judie Choate and Steve Poole, Bill Burback and Peter Hofmann, Carol and Jerry Prueitt, Meghan Day Healey, Carole and Frank Lalli, Geny Phillips, Jont Enroth, Aris Mixon, Bonnie Mulville of April 56, Steve Liewald of Kurt Adler-Santa's World, Carol Kappenhagen of Gracious Home, Brenda Hildenbrand of McAdoo Rugs, Howard and Joan Basis of Olde Antiques, Joyce and Don Coffman of Coffman's Antiques, Barbara Singer of The Birdhouse Gallery, The Different Drummer's Kitchen, and the Sweet family of Sweet's Tree Farm. A thank you to Germana Sachs of Mazzeo's Meats and the team at Masse's fishmonger, both at Guido's Marketplace in Great Barrington. A special thanks to Joan Turner and Kevin Lahey of The Main Course in Garrison, New York, for preparing my poached pear recipe that looks so beautiful on the cover of the book. To the children who created the drawings on page 107—Mitchell and Melissa Feigeles, Canada Choate, Hannah and Meredith Lee, and the "big kid" Julie Feigeles—a great big thanks and holiday hug!

A collection of Belsnichols, the dour faced and stern version of Santa Claus that doled out punishments as well as rewards for children at Christmas, are arranged around an antique feather tree complete with its miniature ornaments and dates from 1880 to 1900. The oldest St. Nick, (far left bottom row), is from the 1870s, the figure mounted on a reindeer is a candy container and dates from 1900 to 1910, and the Santa with his sleigh was also meant to hold candy treats and is from the 1920s.

INTRODUCTION

—✦—

At Christmas play and make good cheer,
For Christmas comes but once a year.

—Thomas Tusser c.1524–1580 from *A Hundred Good Points of Husbandry* (1557, *The Farmer's Daily Diet*)

THE ONLY THING I HAVE EVER FOUND REGRETTABLE about Christmas is that it *does* only come "but once a year." Fortunately, however, it is a holiday that can be celebrated and enjoyed as a season made up of many days, not just one. So I have always taken advantage of every one of the twelve and more days of Christmas because nothing brings me as much joy and pleasure as its spirit, traditions, and festivities.

My father used to say that my face lit up like a Christmas tree just at the mention of that holiday, and would teasingly threaten to pinch my cheek to see if that would make me twinkle just like some tree lights do. My mother claimed that I had "visions of sugar plums dancing in my head," explaining why I just couldn't keep still the entire month of December. Even my big brother understood how special Christmas and all its traditions were to me and never, never revealed that there "was no Santa Claus"— even when I demanded to know the truth. Family conventional wisdom chalked up my total enthrallment to the fact that I was meant

This is the stocking my parents had embroidered with my name and put out for Santa to fill on my first Christmas. I've used it every year since. A little worse for wear, the snow white trim and printed scene are now cream-colored with age.

to be a Christmas baby, due to arrive in this world around the twenty-fifth of December. But I missed that Christmas, arriving nine days late—saving me from the fate of being named Noel or Holly.

As with every small child, my initial focus was on the excitement of the colorfully wrapped presents with the surprises they contained, the over-stuffed stockings filled with treats, and the glitter and dazzle of the ornaments suspended on the tree. On Christmas morning I was amazed at the magical world that my parents, Santa, and the elves had created in our living room—I was like Dorothy entering the Emerald City in *The Wizard of Oz*. I wanted to make magic like this too, and did so as soon as I was capable.

In my childhood home, holiday preparations began early and only finished on Christmas Eve. It was a time that bustled with happy activity and purpose. A division of labor between my parents initiated certain traditions that are now cherished memories.

It was Mom who took me to see Santa Claus at Macy's and "sent" my letter to him— she kept one, which I now have. While my mother addressed her greeting cards, I made mine with the supply of craft paper and stick-on stars we purchased together for that purpose. Upon her return from work in the evening on the twenty-fourth, the painstaking task of putting tinsel on the tree fell to her deft hands—as did the privilege of setting up the Nativity scene, which was hers alone. My father read Christmas stories to me and took me to see the tree at Rockefeller Center. And Dad and I were in charge of our tree. I remember bringing down the boxes of ornaments and hanging the decorations as a quiet and concentrated time spent together only occasionally interrupted by a dispute over the placement of a ball or our singing a carol.

The selection of the tree, however, was quite another matter. There would be tension in the air even as we set out on our quest, my mother's words echoing around us—"Listen to your father, Linda. And no arguments. Nothing too big this time!" But each year those words were put aside when my pleadings of "Please, please, Daddy, this one. It's so perfect and beautiful" would dissipate his resolve. So every Christmas we'd arrive home with a tree too tall and often too broad for our small apartment. It became a family tradition that the first part of trimming the tree always got under way with a saw.

In the months before my husband and I shared our first Christmas, my father offered him some words of warning and advice: "Watch out for the tree" and "Be firm." In the years that followed, Michel and I have carried on the big tree custom, just as we have continued to observe and honor many other holiday traditions taken from both our families that bring the spirit of Christmas to life each year. In our house we go in for a big Christmas in a big way.

This book is offered as a celebration of the joys of Christmas I've long delighted in with family and friends—whether gathered together at the table, around the tree, in church, or out caroling. While the feasts of the Christmas table created with these eight menus can provide truly special dishes that will come together as memorable and pleasurable holiday lunches and dinners, they are meant as just the starting points. With each menu aspects of the origins or history of different Christmas traditions and customs are presented to enrich our understanding of this wonderful time of year. As many of these traditions have found their expression in creative design as artful objects, these too are discussed and shown, many of them antique collectibles. And finally, to capture the magic of Christmas and make it materialize in our homes—just as my parents did in my childhood home—those holiday customs and objects are explored as decorating themes for the house, as well as the festive table.

In making Christmas meaningful, merry, and bright for those around us, we create the best gift anyone can give or receive: joy. It's a shame it comes but once a year—so, in the words of John Greenleaf Whittier (1807–1892):

Somehow not only for Christmas
But all the long year through,
The joy that you give to others
Is the joy that comes back to you

My very best wishes for a Merry Christmas. . . all the year long.

Linda Arnaud

Heavenly Party

HORS D'OEUVRES
Tomato Tartlets and Asparagus Tartlets
Crab and Smoked Trout Pâté with Toasts

•

STARTER
Christmas "Vichyssoise"

•

MAIN COURSE
Fresh Ham with Maple-Walnut Cranberry Glaze
Turkey Breast Stuffed with Apples, Cinnamon, and Thyme

•

SIDE DISHES
Twice-Baked Potato and Yam Cups
Grape Tomato, Broccoli, and Cauliflower Salad
Cranberry Sauces

Reisling and Bourgogne Aligote
Shiraz and Merlot

•

DESSERT
Angel's Christmas Layer Cake

Gruet Blanc de Noir Methode Champenoise

Angels we have heard on high . . . sweetly singing o'er the plains

ALTHOUGH I USUALLY PREFER GIVING SMALL DINNER parties rather than large gatherings, I do enjoy hosting something on a slightly grander scale on occasion—if it's a very special one. The Christmas holiday period is certainly a perfect time to consider pulling out the stops for a special party for friends. Because everyone's calendar is full of social engagements in December, setting an early date for the gathering is a good idea. And the food and the setting should be fitting for a party that guests will remember as "simply heavenly."

In working out the menu, the practical aspects of preparing the dishes and serving to a large group, with the facilities available in my home, are taken into account. While focusing on seasonal favorites or treats, I try to choose those that can be prepared or completed in advance.

As the party will be a buffet, involving a few tables set up for serving, using decorations with a specific color and design theme gives them visual unity, as well as festivity.

MENU: For a buffet meant to serve many, it's a good idea to offer a choice for the meats served as the main course to accommodate any guests with strong food preferences. While a fresh ham is always a perfect way to feed and please a crowd—it is festive, flavorful, and economical—adding a poultry dish to the menu should take care of most tastes. Choose the traditional holiday bird, turkey, but roast just the breast, boned, rolled, and stuffed with something delicious. The turkey rolled around the stuffing will look beautiful when sliced and arranged on a platter. These two meat dishes are perfect for parties: they can be cooked in advance, carved in the kitchen, and attractively presented, ready for self-service at the buffet table.

The side dishes are also host-friendly, as they can be prepared in advance and finished just before serving. A combination of blanched or lightly cooked vegetables of contrasting colors makes an interesting salad to serve alongside a traditional green salad. The potato and yam puree is appealing, piped into individual serving cups made from the potato skins.

The creamy vichyssoise is my savory alternative to the traditional sweet eggnog served in punch bowls at holiday parties. Have your guests sip their soup from punch bowl glasses or elegant china coffee cups for a festive touch—and for ease in buffet dining.

The grand finale for a festive buffet dinner is the dessert, and it should look as special as it tastes. The angel's

cake carries out the party's festive theme, with its Christmas red and green layers and cloud-white icing, while providing a sweet ending to the evening.

TABLE AND DECORATIONS: *A*ngels of all descriptions, stars of all shapes and sizes, and the Nativity scene are the chosen holiday motifs to give the party its festive theme. Linens, glassware, and china as well as Christmas decorations and ornaments are selected in the lavish color scheme of varying shades of gold and red—unifying the decorations of the room and various serving tables.

TRADITIONS: *T*he Christmas story tells of the birth of Christ in a stable in the city of Bethlehem. The barn animals, shepherds with their flocks from the nearby fields, the Wise Men from the East, and angels are present to honor the newborn child and his parents.

This central scene and these characters of the Christmas narrative are well-known to many of us and have been represented in paintings and three-dimensional figures for centuries in works of folk art, as well as in famous masterpieces. On a quite personal level, the Nativity scene comes to us in the form of seasonal greeting cards and the miniature replica of the scene—called a crèche—often found by the Christmas tree in our homes.

*F*rom the nineteenth century, the elements to make or add to the Nativity scene that would be set up in the home were widely available at affordable prices from the crib markets in Germany. In the twentieth century, the key figures and building could be bought in a packaged manger set—additional figures could be added later.

While sculptural representations of the Christ Child in the crib may date to as early as the mid–sixth century, history suggests that the tradition of the three-dimensional crèche scene originated with St. Francis of Assisi in 1223. The Italian monk created a living tableau of the Nativity setting as part of Christmas celebrations, positioning an ox and an ass in a manger strewn with hay; the other characters were omitted and their presence was left to spiritual imagination. The clergy adopted and adapted St. Francis's idea, finding it an effective means of communicating the story of Christmas to the illiterate.

The scenes grew in concept to include all the personages and, over time, were set up in homes as well as in churches. The grand dwellings of the nobility featured Nativity scenes of an elaborate if not grandiose scale and style. Figures were often large, beautifully rendered, and lavishly dressed. Precious materials were used as decorative accents, and clockwork mechanisms sometimes provided music and movement. Tableaux of the Nativity could sometimes occupy an entire floor of a princely residence.

Angels' association with the Nativity scene is found in the New Testament, while the origins of angels can be traced to the myths and religions of ancient Greece and Rome, as well as to Judaic traditions. Winged creatures of human form, they are messengers of the gods or God's word and can act as guardians to man. As noted in so many Christmas carols, angels announce the birth of Christ to the world in their role as bearers of good tidings to the soul.

COLLECTIBLES: *M*any of the nobility became collectors of the Italian-made, moulded terra-cotta crèche figures, and the more refined wax or carved wood ones produced in Germany—figures produced in glass and white faience were also appreciated. Only the wealthy could enjoy the sophisticated and artistically executed figures, as they were expensive. For the poor and the less affluent classes, there were rough wood-carved and pipe clay figures, and others fashioned in dough, composition, or papier-mâché. These folk art crèche figures were widely available at Christmas fairs and street markets, where families would go to purchase new additions each year. The Nativity tradition was popularized with the addition of figures of local colorful personages—of particular note are the world famous clay Santons produced in the south of France at the beginning of the nineteenth century. As the Christmas manger display grew to incorporate more and more secular characters, the background settings expanded from the manger and Bethlehem to local locales. German Christmas mountains and later American Putz scenes are the precursors of those snow villages we may have set up as children (see page 143 for more about these villages).

Setting up the manger has continued as a Christmas custom into the twenty-first century. For families, the crèche is considered an heirloom to be cherished and passed on; for others, it represents a world of collectible miniatures treasured for their age or art.

Figures of angels were produced for Nativity scenes from the outset, and their development parallels that of the other crèche characters. However, the angel figures made for the Christmas crib markets soon appeared in homes, hung on the tree as well as part of the manger arrangement. Angel tree ornaments made of gold foil, wax, papier-mâché, and cut-out paper were much sought after. The physical characteristics of Christmas angels were transformed by the German tradition of the Christkindl and the Protestant opposition to the use of religious imagery. Seen as Christ's spiritual messenger and the gift-giver for children, the Christkindl is pictured as a fair-haired, winged child robed in white—an angelic image more widely used for paper scrap or cards than for tree ornaments. Angels were given less heavenly connections in British and U.S. markets, and were restyled as tree fairies or Christmas dolls, clothed in dresses rather than robes and bearing a magic wand.

A Christmas party for a large group deserves a setting decorated on a grand scale. The evening's theme of a "Heavenly Party" offers a wealth of ideas for the type of holiday decorations that provide a festive backdrop to the celebration. The angels who announced the birth of Christ to the shepherds in their fields and the star that led the Three Wise Men to the birthplace in Bethlehem are the celestial entities traditionally associated with the celebration of Christmas, and particularly with the visualization of the Christmas story or Nativity scene, called a crèche. A color theme of rich Christmas red and glittering metallic golds unify the setting, the tableware and the story.

Some of the built-in shelves that hold books and bric-a-brac the year round are cleared for the Christmas story display and become the focal point for the party's theme. The Arnaud family's crèche—which has been used every Christmas since the late 1950s—a host of angels collected over the years, a skyful of stars that were made to top or hang from holiday trees or were home-made for this occasion, and some of the gold decorated china that will be used during the party fill the large niches that are framed by streamers of star studded red velvet ribbon.

The china and silverware are being set up on the red draped table for the buffet service. A carved angel and gold foil tree were chosen as the table's centerpiece instead of a floral arrangement. The tree's ornaments, in varying shades and finishes of gold, are larger in size than would be normally used for its table top size to create an opulent effect.

Tomato Tartlets
and Asparagus Tartlets

———✦———

Use the Short Crust Pastry Dough recipe on page 159 in "The Pantry." The recipe will provide enough to make 40 tartlets; the cream recipe is enough to fill them. The vegetable ingredients make 20 of each. You will need 40 fluted non-stick tartlet molds (2¼-inch diameter by ¾-inch deep).

For the Tomato Filling

 1 tablespoon extra-virgin olive oil

 2 tablespoons finely chopped shallots

 ½ teaspoon finely chopped garlic

 10 grape tomatoes

 Pinch of sea salt

 Freshly ground black pepper

For the Asparagus Filling

 1 tablespoon extra-virgin olive oil

 2 tablespoons finely chopped shallots

 20 asparagus tips, cooked (see page 156)

 Pinch of sea salt

 Freshly ground black pepper

 1 tablespoon finely chopped cilantro

For the Tartlets

 Flour and butter for the tartlet molds

 1 recipe Short Crust Pastry Dough (page 159)

 2 large eggs

 1½ cups whole milk

 ½ cup heavy cream

 ¼ teaspoon sea salt

Freshly ground black pepper

½ cup shredded cheese (Gruyére, Swiss, or sharp cheddar)

7 anchovy fillets, rinsed and cut into thirds

7 oil-cured Moroccan black olives, pitted and cut into thirds

MAKE THE TOMATO FILLING: Heat the oil in a sauté pan over medium-low heat, add the shallots and garlic, and cook for 2 to 3 minutes, until the shallots are translucent. Add the tomatoes, season with salt and pepper, and cook, turning and tossing for 2 to 3 minutes, until the tomatoes begin to show orange spots on their skin. Immediately remove the pan from the heat and transfer the tomatoes to a small bowl to cool. Set aside.

MAKE THE ASPARAGUS FILLING: Heat the oil in a sauté pan over medium-low heat, add the shallots, and cook for 2 to 3 minutes, until they are translucent. Add the asparagus, season with salt and pepper, and cook, tossing, for 1 minute. Immediately remove the pan from the heat and transfer to a bowl. Sprinkle the cilantro over the asparagus and stir gently to combine. Set aside.

MAKE THE TARTLETS: Preheat the oven to 400°F, setting the rack at the middle level.

Grease 40 tartlet molds with butter, then lightly dust the molds, rolling pin, and work surface with flour.

Cut the pastry dough into 40 small pieces and shape them into balls. Roll out each ball into a circle, ⅛-inch thick, and fit the circles into the molds. Trim the top edges of the molds and arrange them on baking sheets.

Cut each tomato in half, and place a tomato half in the center of each of 20 molds; place an asparagus tip in each of the remaining molds. Set aside.

Combine the eggs, milk, cream, and salt and pepper in a mixing bowl and, using an electric hand mixer or a wire whisk, beat the mixture until frothy. Divide the cream mixture among the tartlet molds, spooning it over the tomatoes or asparagus until the molds are almost full. Sprinkle the cheese over the filled molds.

Place the baking sheet with the tartlets in the oven and bake for 25 to 30 minutes, until the crusts are golden and the centers are set. Remove from the oven and allow the tartlets to cool. Turn the tartlets out of the molds, garnish the tomato ones with the anchovies and the asparagus ones with the olives, and arrange on a serving dish. Serve at room temperature or cooler.

OPPOSITE: *As the dinner will be a buffet service, the china and silverware are set out on the main table from which the guests will help themselves. The plates for the different courses are stacked and arranged around the table. Wrapping up the knife and fork in a large, lap-sized napkin, which provides perfect protection for dining buffet style, is a tidy and attractive alternative to the clutter of loose cutlery on the serving table. I've tied up the napkins with a fancy red and gold braid accented by silky red tassels and presented them in an antique red glass tray with a leaf motif detailed iron handle that echoes the design of the ruby glass decanter behind.*

ABOVE: *An assortment of cut, pressed, and blown glass decanters are part of my antique glassware collection that is put to perfect use for the self-service bar arranged on a small table decorated with golden angels, stars and cut crystal ice bucket filled with gold ornaments.*

Decanting the red and white wines and nonalcoholic beverages being served at the party will save space, and add a touch of elegance.

Crab and Smoked Trout Pâté with Toasts

I tasted a shrimp and trout version of this at a cocktail party, but when I first attempted to reproduce what I had tasted, I made use of some leftover crab I had on hand. This makes a lovely spread for plain or toasted breads and crackers, but is equally good when used as a filling, as in the recipe for Smoked Salmon Parcels and Cucumber Maki Rolls (page 146), or spooned onto endive leaves. You can prepare the spread up to 2 days ahead; keep it in an airtight container in the refrigerator.

> ¾ pound lump crabmeat, picked over for shells and broken up with a fork
>
> 1 to 1¼ pounds smoked trout filets, boned, skinned, and broken into small pieces
>
> 1 pound cream cheese, at room temperature, cut into small pieces
>
> ½ cup finely chopped chives
>
> 4 tablespoons brined capers, rinsed and drained
>
> 2 teaspoons lemon juice
>
> Small loaf of bread (at least 20 slices), crust trimmed off, cut into 2-inch circles; or toasted bread circles or triangles

Combine the crabmeat and trout in the bowl of a food processor and process until finely chopped. Add the cream cheese and process until the mixture is a smooth, thick paste. Transfer the mixture to an attractive serving bowl and stir in the chives, capers, and lemon juice until well blended. Serve at room temperature alongside a basket of bread, toasts, or crackers.

Christmas "Vichyssoise"

———✦———

$\mathcal{A}$ few of the glittering golden ornaments on the tabletop tree are worth their weight in gold—and more. These are the gilded papier-mâché and embossed card ornaments that were molded as three-dimensional designs or pressed flat silhouettes most commonly produced in the form of shells (above and below), animals, birds, musical instruments and angels or fairies called Dresdens. Good quality Dresdens show very fine detailing in their designs and have been much sought after since they were first made in Germany in the 1870s. As these delicate ornaments were only produced for some 40 years, and are some of the most popular of Christmas collectibles, they are hard to come by today.

$\mathcal{S}$erve this chilled leek, potato, and sweet potato soup in punch glasses or elegant china coffee cups—think of it as a savory eggnog! Have a fancy salt cellar or antique sugar shaker of nutmeg available for guests to add a sprinkling of that classic Christmas flavor, and offer a bowl of chopped fresh chives as well.

This recipe yields six to eight portions when served in traditional soup bowls. For this menu, it will serve a glass or coffee-cupful per person, with some left over for seconds. The recipe can be doubled to serve more substantial portions.

4 tablespoons unsalted butter

4 to 5 medium leeks, thoroughly washed, thinly sliced, white and light green parts

1 to 1¼ pounds boiling potatoes, peeled and coarsely chopped

½ pound white sweet potatoes, peeled and coarsely chopped

2 quarts good-quality chicken broth

1 teaspoon sea salt

Freshly ground white pepper

1½ cups heavy cream

½ cup chopped chives

Ground nutmeg

Melt the butter in a large saucepan over medium heat, add the leeks, and stir until well coated with the butter. Add the potatoes and sweet potatoes and stir until they glisten with the butter coating. Pour in the broth, season with salt and white pepper, and cook at a gentle simmer for 45 minutes, or until the vegetables are quite tender—until the potatoes can be easily pierced with the point of a knife. Press the contents of the pot through a food mill into a large bowl and season to taste with salt and white pepper if desired. (The recipe can be prepared in advance up to this point and kept refrigerated for 1 to 2 days. To save storage space, transfer the soup to a tall plastic airtight container.)

Transfer the soup to a large serving bowl or tureen, stir in the cream, and refrigerate for a few hours, until cold. Serve chilled.

Fresh Ham with Maple-Walnut Cranberry Glaze

For this menu serve the ham with one or two turkey breasts, depending on the size of the ham and the appetites of your friends. But don't forget: the leftover ham works in myriad ways for some time after the party.

Note: All the roasted meat recipes in this book were cooked using a Polder Thermo-Timer. The thermometer probe is inserted into the meat before cooking begins and stays in place throughout the cooking, attached by a wire to a temperature read-out panel outside the oven; the oven door can still close tightly. The obvious advantage is that this allows you to closely monitor the roast's temperature without opening the oven door and affecting the oven's temperature and the cooking time of the meat. The result is a perfectly cooked roast every time. This is a Christmas stocking stuffer that is sure to please. I treasure mine so much I should keep it in a velvet-lined box. (See "Sources," page 163.)

The Maple-Walnut Cranberry Sauce can serve as an accompaniment as well as a glaze.

For the Glaze

- 1 cup pureed Maple-Walnut Cranberry Sauce (page 155)
- ¼ cup cranberry juice
- 2 tablespoons maple syrup
- 2 tablespoons honey
- ½ teaspoon sea salt
- Freshly ground black pepper

The narrative of the Christmas story represented in three-dimensional form is well-known to many of us, particularly familiar are the crèche replicas we display near the Christmas tree in our homes.

While St. Francis of Assisi's creation in 1223 of the Nativity scene as a living tableau with an ox and ass in a manger may have been one of the earliest example of these, the lavish and large nativities found in the homes of the rich in the seventeenth and eighteenth centuries were the most extravagant. Artistic workmanship, precious materials and mechanisms that could provide music and motion were characteristic of the crèches of the nobility and could take up a floor of their residence. Today's family crèche is likely to be more in the style of the creations produced for the popular Christmas or crib markets at less dear prices. The Arnaud heirloom family crèche (opposite bottom) reflects the familiar and centuries old tradition and style—though made in the 1950s. A crib scene set within the 1970s Provençal pottery jug (opposite top) is from the tradition of the French Santons figures that included personages of local color. The seed pod figures (below) from Guatemala capture the essence of a primitive folk art and crafts style.

For the Ham

18- to 23-pound fresh ham on the bone, trimmed of tough outer skin

5 cups kosher or coarse sea salt

Freshly cracked black pepper

8 cloves garlic, peeled and thinly sliced

MAKE THE GLAZE: Puree the cup of cranberry sauce in bowl of a food processor. Add the cranberry juice, maple syrup, honey, and salt and pepper and process until combined. (The glaze can be prepared 2 to 3 days in advance and stored in the refrigerator. Bring to room temperature before using.)

MAKE THE HAM: Place the ham in a very large plastic bucket or tub, or in a kitchen work sink, fill with water to cover, and pour in 5 cups salt. After 6 hours, remove the ham from its brining bath, rinse well, and pat dry. Season with pepper. Set aside.

Preheat the oven to 325°F, setting the rack at the lowest level.

Place the ham in a heavy foil-lined roasting pan. Make small incisions all over the ham with the point of a small knife, and insert garlic slices into the incisions. Generously coat the ham with the cranberry glaze. Insert the meat thermometer in the middle section of the ham, but not touching the bone; follow the manufacturer's instructions for setting the temperature timer to 155°F.

Set the roasting pan with the ham in the oven, with the exterior thermometer panel on the outside. Bake for 1 hour, then tent with a piece of aluminum foil. Continue to bake until the thermometer reads 155°F, another 5 to 6 hours. Remove the ham from the oven and let rest for about 20 minutes before carving. (If you're preparing the ham a day or longer in advance, refrigerate. Bring to room temperature and then reheat, covered with foil, in a warm oven for 1 to 2 hours. Let rest for about 20 minutes, then serve warm or at room temperature.)

Turkey Breast Stuffed with Apples, Cinnamon, and Thyme

Serve the stuffed turkey breast with a cranberry sauce such as the Pear-Ginger Cranberry Sauce on page 155 in "The Pantry."

1 or 2 tart apples, peeled, cored, and chopped

¼ cup parsley

1 teaspoon ground cinnamon

1 teaspoon finely chopped thyme leaves, plus additional whole leaves

2 tablespoons finely chopped garlic

4-pound whole turkey breast, boned and butterflied (skin left on)

Sea salt

Freshly ground black pepper

¾ cup unseasoned fine bread crumbs

Extra-virgin olive oil

2 tablespoons vegetable oil

½ cup good-quality chicken broth

Preheat the oven to 400°F, setting the rack at the middle level.

Combine the apples, parsley, cinnamon, chopped thyme, and garlic in a bowl and mix well.

Lay the turkey breast, skin side down, on a cutting board and pound the meat all over with a mallet to flatten it. Remove excess fatty pieces and tough muscle or tenders. Season with salt and pepper, sprinkle with half of the bread crumbs, and spoon the apple mixture over, distributing it evenly but leaving a ½-inch border all around. Sprinkle with the remaining bread crumbs.

Draw up both ends of the meat on the long side so they overlap slightly in the middle and secure along the length with a few bamboo skewers. Then tie up the breast with kitchen twine, securing the roll every inch. Brush the turkey all over with olive oil, and season with salt and pepper and thyme leaves.

As they announce the birth of Christ to the world, figures of angels were created for Nativity scenes from their beginning, and quickly appeared as ornaments for the tree. Tree angels were made for the Christmas crib markets—as were the crèches—and were popular in gold foil, wax, papier-mâché and paper cutouts.

Crèche and tree angels of greater artistic quality were created for the church and the rich. Those of eighteenth-century Italy are often imitated today in mass-produced versions of considerable beauty.

The gilt, wood-carved angel figure (opposite), is Italian from the eighteenth century.

Angel musicians, depicted playing their instruments, have been popular with all artists over the centuries. Paintings and figurines feature these celestial beings making heavenly music to herald Christ's birth (below).

Heat the vegetable oil in a large skillet over high heat, add the turkey, and cook until just browned on all sides. Remove from the skillet.

Insert the meat thermometer and set timer to 160°F. Place in a foil-lined roasting pan and set the pan in the oven. Bake for 25 minutes, then baste with broth and continue to cook for another 25 to 35 minutes, until the thermometer reads 160°F. Remove from the oven, transfer to a cutting board or platter, and let the roast rest for 15 to 20 minutes before carving. Serve warm or room temperature.

(The turkey breast can be prepared up to this point 1 day in advance and refrigerated. Bring to room temperature, then rewarm and serve.)

The china used here is the favorite classic patterned porcelain "Wedding Band"—a plain pure white china edged and trimmed with bands of gold. At the height of its popularity in the nineteenth century, it served as the everyday china for American presidents and the upper middle class. An export product of Limoges, France, it was shipped here in an undecorated state to avoid certain tariff laws. The finishing touches of gold were applied to the fired and glazed china by American artisans afterward.

Interestingly, there is no single style of shape or design for the decoration for this tableware, so collectors are often open to mixing different gold designs, tones of white, shapes, and even old with new. "Old Paris porcelain," as it is also called, is still made today as high quality china and inexpensive imports, while antique pieces are reasonably priced—making it quite accessible. As most catering equipment rental sources offer a gold-edged dinnerware, adding pieces needed for a party is easy if you mix.

The cups of the coffee service (above) in the niche have nine different gold patterns. The plates on the table (right)—with the stuffed turkey, potato cup and salad—yet another. Angels and stars meant for the tree are the holiday decorations for the "heavenly" theme.

Twice-Baked Potato and Yam Cups

Horseradish makes this dish a tangy taste contrast to the sweet glazed ham and fruit-stuffed turkey breast. It's also a natural combination with a roasted tenderloin of beef or grilled steaks after the holiday season.

To arrive at 1 potato cup per person, use 1 potato for every 2 people. When the yam and other ingredients are added to create the filling, you'll have enough filling to overstuff 16 potato cups or to save for later.

> 8 to 10 baking potatoes, washed and patted dry
> 4 yams (about 1½ pounds), washed and patted dry
> ¾ cup unsalted butter
> 20 ounces crème fraîche or sour cream
> ½ cup prepared horseradish, drained
> Sea salt
> Freshly ground black pepper
> Paprika
> Fresh parsley

Preheat the oven to 400°F, setting the rack at the middle level.

With a fork, prick the potatoes and the yams a few times all over. Set them on the rack in the oven and bake for 50 minutes, until they're soft when gently squeezed using an oven mitt. Remove from the oven and let cool for a few minutes. Leave the oven on if you're serving the potatoes directly.

Peel the yams, cut into dice, and put them in a large mixing bowl.

Cut the potatoes in half horizontally. Gently and carefully, so as not to tear the skin, scoop out the potato flesh—leaving a coating of potato on the inside of the skins—and add it to the yams in the bowl. Set the skins, or "cups," open side up, in a baking dish.

With a potato ricer, mash the yams, potatoes, and butter together in a bowl until well blended. Add the crème fraîche and horseradish and continue to mash to a purée consistency. Season with salt and pepper.

Fill each potato cup with some of the mixture, spooning it in or piping it in using a pastry bag with a large tip. (The cups can be prepared up to this point a few hours in advance. Refrigerate, then bring to room temperature before finishing.)

Sprinkle each cup with some paprika and put the baking dish in the oven. Bake for 35 to 40 minutes, until the skins are crisp and the topping is golden. Remove from the oven, top each cup with a sprig of parsley, and serve.

Grape Tomato, Broccoli, and Cauliflower Salad

1½ cups Cilantro Vinaigrette (page 155 in "The Pantry")
1½ cups grape tomatoes or small cherry tomato halves
3 heads cauliflower, cut florets into bite-size pieces (page 156 in "The Pantry")
2½ to 2¾ pounds broccoli, cut florets into bite-size pieces (page 157 in "The Pantry")

Pour half of the vinaigrette into a large serving or salad bowl. Add the tomatoes and vegetables and toss. Pour in the rest of the vinaigrette and toss again. Serve.

The Nativity scene has been a popular subject for artists over the centuries. Great works of art depicting the scene of Christ's birth in the manger in Bethlehem that include the Holy Family, the shepherds, the Three Kings and, of course, a host of heavenly angels were commissioned by the church and ruling classes of the day. Many of these have been beautifully reproduced for the seasonal greetings cards we now receive at Christmas. A collection of these cards, along with sprays of golden stars and star ornaments, serves as the setting for a group of angelic musicians that are meant to top the Christmas tree. Angels were often shown with musical instruments and were as popular as the star for topping the Christmas tree.

Angel's Christmas Layer Cake

*T*his sugary traditional sponge cake is festively colored in alternating layers of Christmas red and green, and topped with cloud-white sugar icing. For those with a particularly sweet tooth it's just heavenly. Offer fresh fruit—like berries, grapes, and clementines—as an alternative, and chocolate truffles to go with coffee.

If you're short on time, buy a good-quality sponge cake mix, follow the instructions, and add the food coloring to the batter. Use any white frosting.

Note: You will need to make 4 cake layers: 2 red and 2 green. To ensure that the 4 layers are exactly the same size, the batter is made individually for each. Double the ingredients if you wish to make the 2 layers of one color at the same time.

For 1 layer of sponge cake:

8 tablespoons unsalted butter (at room temperature), plus additional for the pan

½ cup self-rising flour, sifted, plus additional for the pan

1 teaspoon baking powder

½ cup superfine sugar

2 large eggs

¼ teaspoon vanilla extract

1 tablespoon food coloring (red or green)

For the icing:

5 teaspoons cream of tartar

5 tablespoons light corn syrup

5 large egg whites

7½ cups confectioners' sugar, sifted

MAKE THE SPONGE CAKE: Preheat the oven to 375°F, setting the rack at the middle level.

Grease a cake pan with butter, dust with flour, and line the bottom with a circle of greaseproof paper.

*A*n angel's cake for the holidays is one with clouds of heavenly white icing and light layers of sponge cake in festive Christmas colors. Stars made from cardboard and sprayed gold are used to decorate the cake, as are the cherub ornaments perched on top and resting on the metallic gold foil base.

The cherub and cherubim are the second order of angels. They are usually depicted as chubby and rosy-faced infants or young children with wings, but often they appear bodiless—their cherubic smiling faces set on wings. Cherubs were most popular as Christmas tree decorations, and were frequently depicted in Victorian Christmas greeting cards, as well as printed scrap for beautiful Victorian albums that are highly prized by collectors.

Combine the butter, flour, baking powder, superfine sugar, eggs, and vanilla in a food processor and blend until thoroughly mixed. Add the food coloring and blend until the batter is a uniform color.

Pour the batter into the prepared pan and level off the top. Bake for 20 minutes or until the cake has risen and pulled away from the sides of the pan.

Remove from the oven and let sit for about 30 seconds, then turn the cake out onto a wire rack to cool. Repeat the process for the remaining 3 layers.

MAKE THE ICING: Combine the cream of tartar, corn syrup, 9 tablespoons water, and the egg whites in a heat-resistant bowl. Using an electric hand mixer, blend the ingredients together, then gradually beat in the confectioners' sugar. Place the bowl on top of a saucepan of simmering water—the bowl should not touch the water. Beat until the mixture becomes thick and forms soft peaks.

Remove the bowl from the heat immediately, but continue beating until the mixture cools; it should still hold soft peaks. Use the icing immediately, working quickly.

ASSEMBLE THE CAKE: Place a green sponge layer on a cake base that will be used for serving, and ice the top. Place a red sponge layer on top, ice it, and continue to layer sponge and icing, ending with a red layer. Then ice the sides and top and create cloud-like sweeps all over the cake. Decorate with gold stars and cherubs.

A festive CHRISTMAS!

With the Compliments of the SEASON

Christmas Wishes

bring Joy to

Let Christmas

THIS "KITTY" BRINGS MY NEW YEAR'S GRE

A Very Happy Christmas

Sweetest music is the greeting
"Merry Christmas" which we heer
This, the happy time of meeting
We shall ever hold most dear.

Christmas Eve Dinner

SERVES 10

HORS D'OEUVRES
Borscht

Sautéed Spicy Shrimp

Oysters with Lemon

Caviar with Toasts

·

STARTER
Sea Scallops with Red Lettuces and Warm Vinaigrette

CHABLIS PREMIER CRU

·

MAIN COURSE
*Roasted Butterflied Whole Salmon with Sour Cream
and Chive Dressing*

·

SIDES
Pirogi

Slow-Cooked Leeks

Asparagus

MEURSAULT

·

DESSERTS
Light-as-a-Feather Cheesecake

Fresh Mixed Berries

VOUVRAY

It came upon a midnight clear,

that glorious song of old . . .

UNLIKE THE HOUSE IN THE FAMOUS CHRISTMAS POEM where not a creature stirs, there are many homes that bustle with the activity of a special celebration on the night before Christmas. In many families, Christmas Eve is observed as an occasion that is as important as the following day. A traditional dinner that incorporates the religious fasting required for that day is followed by midnight mass and then, in some families, the opening of presents.

My husband remembers the excitement and festivities of Christmas Eve, or *Réveillon* as it is known in France, closely rivaling that of Christmas Day in his early childhood home. The word *Réveillon* refers to both Christmas Eve and New Year's Eve. The Arnaud table was beautifully set, aglow with flickering candlelight and laden with extra-special dishes. While they began their celebrations with a late dinner around ten in the evening, in other homes, and even in restaurants, the festivities would not start until after Midnight Mass.

When I married into his French family, I adopted their custom of marking the occasion of December 24 with a special dinner and festive table. However, the feast I created for us added elements from my Ukrainian family's celebration of Christmas Eve. As a child, I thought myself very fortunate to have two Christmases—one on December 25 and the other on January 7. Our second Christmas consisted of a ritual dinner prepared by my grandmother and her sisters, which took place on the night of January 6. Although there were no wrapped presents exchanged at this second Christmas, the many special dishes that were time-consuming to prepare and that appeared on our tables only once or twice a year were regarded as wonderful gifts and received with appreciation and delight.

Combining a little of each of our families' traditions, Michel and I celebrate a Christmas Eve of our own, one that preserves some of our fondest childhood memories and treats.

MENU: *W*hile both the French and Ukrainian family dinners dictated a meatless menu consisting of many courses, the latter required that no dishes contain dairy products and that there be twelve dishes served—one for each of the twelve Apostles.

This menu is meatless (but not dairy-free) and offers twelve dishes (cheating a bit by counting the sour cream

dressing for the salmon—I've found that serving anything more is a bit too much). Keeping that in mind, many of the recipe quantities are scaled down in their portions, balanced to the serving of so many dishes.

The oysters and caviar are a traditional French treat, as are the sea scallops—an Arnaud family favorite. Here the oysters and caviar are served with the aperitifs, along with a very traditional peasant soup, borscht. Offering the soup in demitasse or small teacups gives it an elegant and festive air—and ensures that the portions will not be too filling in the context of this extensive menu. So are the portions for the leeks and asparagus scaled down in serving size to 2 thin or 1 thick leek and 2 asparagus per person.

Serving a whole fish at the table is as festive as the traditional holiday bird. Salmon is the fish of choice for many, preferred for its taste and its size, large enough to serve many. My grandmother's pirogi were the highlight of our Christmas Eve for me, so this dinner wouldn't be right without a version of them. They are served along with leeks and asparagus to accompany the fish. The sour cream sauce offers a dressing that works for both the salmon and the pirogis.

Two desserts complete the twelve dishes: fresh mixed berries are a delicious contrast to the cheesecake.

TABLE AND DECORATIONS: *A*n old-fashioned Christmas is the theme for the candlelight dinner that will last until near midnight. The look is as romantic as the images of Christmas presented on the Victorian greeting cards that are used as decorations for the table and sideboard, while much of the tableware and linens are faithful to the style of the period. Some do date from the last few decades of the nineteenth century.

As the menu particularly features seafood, a Victorian fish-motif china and ocean-themed silver service are used for the table setting. Natural seashells and shell-motif pottery and glassware are used as complementary accents.

TRADITIONS: *T*he discrepancy between dates for the Eastern Orthodox and Western European Christmas is explained by their use of two different calendars. Those religions or cultures that still use the ancient Julian calendar, as established by the Roman emperor Julius Caesar, calculate January 7 as the correct calendar day of Christ's birth. The rest of the world calculates the days of the year, and so Christmas and other religious holidays, by the Gregorian calendar, established by Pope Gregory XIII in 1582 and in common use since that time.

While many of the traditions for Christmas Eve are solely of religious significance, others are more secular. The custom of decorating and lighting up the tree on—and not before—December 24 is one of those. It was part of a tradition that originated in Germany and traveled to other parts of Europe and America. At the royal palace of Queen Victoria, the German ritual of decorating a tree and lighting it on December 24 was introduced by Prince Albert and was strictly adhered to throughout Victoria's long reign. As with many other ideas embraced by the well-loved queen, Victorian society followed suit.

The delivery of gifts for the children on Christmas Eve was originally made by the Christkindl and not Santa. The Christkindl was believed to be a mixture of heavenly being and beautiful child that visited on Christmas Eve to touch our hearts with spiritual love, entering homes through a window left open in anticipation of his visit. In a short time, the spiritual gift became real presents, and eventually the role of the Christkindl came to be played by a fair-haired angelic young girl, dressed in white and often wearing wings, who reenacted the visit for her family.

When the concept of the Christkindl arrived in America, it evolved into the figure of Kriss Kringle—one of the many variations of the character we call Santa Claus.

The Christmas cards we all so dutifully send today are another German creation that became a significant and very widespread custom as early as the middle of the nineteenth century and one that blossomed toward century's end. Seasonal greetings were printed on cards that could be as simple as illustrated postcards or as complicated as three-dimensional die-cut and pop-up cards known as transformation cards, or ornately fringed or cord-piped styles. Recognized artists and illustrators were drawn into this new industry as the seasonal cards grew in popularity. At one time, the season's new cards were reviewed and rated in the press, just like books and paintings. The printed Christmas images for cards were the same types of designs used for gift and candy boxes, product advertising, retail catalogues, calendars, and scrap for souvenir albums—and their styles evolved along with new printing processes as much as with fads or trends.

COLLECTIBLES: *The* printed images of Christmas provide a world of collectibles in a variety of forms. Obviously, the more elaborate or intricate the form, the more detailed the design; and the better the quality of the printing, the more valuable the piece, as are those created by and credited to a well-known artist. Treasure troves and true finds are the Victorian scrapbooks and Christmas card albums in which pieces of scrap, clippings from magazines, chromolithographic prints, and trade or greeting cards would be pasted.

Bells, holly, snowy villages, and figures of children bundled up for a wintery walk were very popular images and symbols of Christmas for Victorian greeting cards (above) and "scrap" (opposite).

Oysters on the Half Shell with Lemon

$\mathcal{M}$y husband's eyes light up at the mention of fresh oysters—morning, noon, or night, he finds them irresistible and prefers to eat them with just a dash of freshly squeezed lemon juice. And although I prefer the pearls they produce to their flesh, oysters are frequently part of special occasions at our table.

As part of an extensive menu like this one, and taking into consideration how many of my guests will most enjoy them, 2 or 3 oysters per person is sufficient to provide "just a taste." If you do not have oyster plates made to hold them securely, present them on a round platter of crushed ice. Have a plate of lemon wedges available, and make sure a bowl for empty shells is handy. Don't serve any oysters whose shells have even slightly opened—throw them out!

To open oysters safely and as easily as possible, I recommend using an oyster knife and oyster glove—or a folded kitchen towel and potholder held in the palm of your hand. The specially designed knife has a thick blade that is strong enough to slice apart the top and bottom shells, and the glove is in a sturdy material to protect against cuts. Clean the oyster shells with cold water and a brush. Then, holding the oyster with the cupped side facing down in the palm of your hand and resting against the oyster glove or padding, slip the blade of the knife into the oyster's hinge and twist the knife to pop off the top shell. Detach the flesh from the top shell, and scoop under the oyster flesh to loosen it from the bottom shell.

Caviar with Toasts

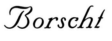

*W*hile oysters were once a "cheap food" and staple of the working-class diet in England until European oyster beds were wiped out by disease, caviar has always been an expensive delicacy. There are many types of caviar—and prices that reflect their relative quality. You can break the bank or choose your favorite from the less expensive varieties: I am terribly fond of salmon roe—and so is my wallet. They have a clean, subtle taste and a refreshing texture, and their bright orange color and size make an attractive presentation in a glass bowl with a small pearl or horn spoon for serving onto small toasted bread squares or miniature biscuits. Serve a bowl of 12 ounces of salmon roe (about $25 to $30), and watch it disappear.

Borscht

*F*amily recipes are treasured, not just for the favorite dishes they produce but for the special memories they are associated with. Almost all the family recipes in my collection will bring to mind a time, a place, or a person while I am preparing them. The recipe for the simple peasant soup borscht, with all its variations seems to span the generations of the Savitsky family. This version, from my mother's cousin's wife, Mary Savitsky, is one I so enjoyed at a recent Christmas Eve celebration at her home. Mary's Ukrainian soup can be finished in two different and equally delicious ways: as a clear broth with the chopped vegetables or as a creamy pureed soup.

(continued)

Because this soup will be sipped from demitasse cups, the puréed version is appropriate here. To serve at another time in bowls with spoons, finish the recipe before straining and separating the broth and vegetables—just remove the bay leaf.

For this menu, a small portion is served in and sipped from demitasse cups as an intermezzo that bridges the change in the taste and pace of the hors d'oeuvres and the starter courses.

2 tablespoons extra-virgin olive oil

1 large onion, peeled and finely chopped

2 celery stalks, finely chopped

2 cloves garlic, finely chopped

¾ cup shredded carrots

¾ cup shredded parsnips

1¼ pounds beets, peeled and julienned

¼ pound mushrooms, cleaned and diced

6 cups vegetable bouillion

1½ cups juice strained from 1 (28-ounce) can peeled tomatoes

1 bay leaf

½ cup sour cream, at room temperature

2 tablespoons finely chopped dill

Heat the oil in a large saucepan, add the onion, celery, garlic, carrots, and parsnips to the pan and cook over medium heat until all the vegetables are soft, 8 to 10 minutes.

Add the beets and mushrooms, cover, and cook for 5 minutes. Pour in the bouillion and juice from the tomatoes, and add the bay leaf. Increase the heat and bring to a boil, then reduce the heat and simmer for 1 hour.

Strain the contents of the saucepan through a sieve into a large bowl and place the vegetables in another bowl. Remove the bay leaf and discard about half of the vegetables.

Pour half the liquid into a blender, add half the remaining vegetables, and blend. Pour the mixture back into the saucepan. Repeat with the remaining liquid and vegetables.

Warm through and serve. Offer some sour cream and dill to top off the soup in their demitasse cups.

Sautéed Spicy Shrimp

This is a year-round favorite at our house, I make it as "the nibbles" for any dinner party. It's so delicious I can hardly get them out of the pan and onto a serving plate before they start to disappear.

2 pounds uncooked medium shrimp (in shells)

For the Marinade
⅓ cup extra-virgin olive oil
3 cloves garlic, finely chopped
2 tablespoons freshly squeezed lime juice
2 or 3 pinches hot red pepper flakes
2 tablespoons finely chopped cilantro
1 tablespoon freshly grated ginger

For the Dipping Sauce
½ cup extra-virgin olive oil
1 clove garlic, pressed
2 tablespoons freshly squeezed lime juice
Pinch hot red pepper flakes (optional)
1 tablespoon finely chopped cilantro

Shell the shrimp and set aside. Combine all the ingredients for the marinade in a non-reactive bowl and add the shrimp. Stir to thoroughly coat the shrimp. Let the shrimp marinate at room temperature for 5 to 10 minutes, but no longer.

Meanwhile, combine all the ingredients for the dipping sauce in a small serving bowl and whisk to blend well. Set aside.

Heat a nonstick wok or sauté pan over medium-high heat, add the shrimp and its marinade, and cook, stirring constantly. Cook for 2 to 3 minutes, until all the shrimp have just turned opaque. Immediately remove the pan from the heat and transfer the shrimp to a serving bowl. Serve hot with the dipping sauce and some toothpicks.

Christmas Eve dinner seems an appropriate occasion for an elegant and romantic setting. A presentation of an old-fashioned look that echoes the beauty of Victorian tables sets off my antique and family heirloom pieces, brought out for the special celebration (see page 39). The crystal shimmers, the silver shines, and the china glows in the flickering candlelight against the background of subtle shadings of antique whites in the layers of lacy table linens. The centerpiece is a folding Victorian Christmas card from Sweden depicting an elaborate Nativity scene in an intricate cut-out design that is handsomely rendered. An antique Russian Father Christmas figure, with snowy beard and thick robe wrapped against the arctic winters, stands close to the center.

As the dinner's focal points are special seafood dishes, I've scattered a collection of sun-bleached seashells around the table and tied sand dollars onto the back of each chair with ribbon—a place card at the front. The modern and Victorian mix with the fish motif china and silver fish service; the classy and the kitsch contrast with the 1950s Baccarat jewel-tone edged crystal wine glasses and the gold and jewel-studded Christmas tree glasses.

Sea Scallops with Red Lettuces and Warm Vinaigrette

⎯⎯※⎯⎯

This dish is best presented on individual plates, so arrange the lettuces before beginning to cook the scallops.

¾ cup Tarragon Vinaigrette, plus additional for serving (page 155 in "The Pantry")

½ pound (2 heads) radicchio, exterior leaves discarded, thinly sliced

½ pound (4 to 5 heads) red endive or radicchio di Treviso or other red-tipped lettuce leaves, separated and washed

10 red radishes, washed, trimmed, and thinly sliced into rounds

2 tablespoons extra-virgin olive oil

2 tablespoons finely chopped shallots

30 large (or 40 small) sea scallops

2 tablespoons red wine vinegar

Pour ¼ cup of the vinaigrette into a mixing bowl, add the radicchio, and toss to coat well.

Divide the endive leaves equally among 10 serving plates and arrange in a fanlike pattern. Place the dressed radicchio and the radishes on the plates on top of the endive ends. Set aside.

Heat the oil in a skillet or sauté pan over medium-high heat and add the shallots; cook until translucent. Add the scallops to the pan, in batches if necessary, and cook for about 2 minutes per side, or until they are golden. Transfer the scallops to a warm plate and loosely cover with foil. Increase the heat under the pan and add the vinegar, scraping up any browned bits with a wooden spoon; cook for 1 minute, or until the vinegar has evaporated. Reduce the heat to low and add the remaining ½ cup vinaigrette; cook for 1 minute. Return the scallops to the pan and cook just long enough to toss and coat with the sauce. Immediately remove the pan from the heat and arrange 3 scallops on each plate of salad. Spoon the pan sauce over the scallops and serve immediately. Pass a pitcher of extra vinaigrette at the table.

In our first house in England, I was surprised to find a bell panel indicating the rooms of the house positioned above the kitchen door—and in the dining room, the sole surviving corresponding buzzer. As the house was neither large nor grand and was built in the 1920s in a modest neighborhood, the idea that servants had been at the original owners' beck and call seemed incongruous. But many of the niceties of formal dining, and the forms they take in table accessories, seem at odds with the way we dine today. Although ringing a dinner bell to call for service may be fruitless, bells are fun to collect and can add a charming touch to a holiday table when patterned with Christmas motifs like the poinsettia here. The use and production of place and menu cardholders became popular in the early twentieth century. And while place cards are seen as quite useful at many dinner parties today, menu cards appear an affectation in most homes. This brass Edwardian holder will add a festive note to the table with its filigree design of a Victorian Christmas scene, even without a menu card.

Roasted Butterflied Whole Salmon with Sour Cream and Chive Dressing

For the Dressing

1½ cups sour cream (not fat free)

3 tablespoons finely chopped chives

For the Salmon

Extra-virgin olive oil

Sea salt

Freshly ground black pepper

6- to 7-pound salmon, butterflied, rinsed, and patted dry

Freshly squeezed lemon juice

Ask your fishmonger to gut, remove the scales, and butterfly the salmon for you (slit down the center, and boned).

MAKE THE DRESSING: Combine the sour cream and chives in a serving bowl until well mixed. Set aside at room temperature.

MAKE THE SALMON: Preheat the oven to 450°F. Line the oven rack with aluminum foil, brush with oil, and sprinkle with salt and pepper. Place the rack in the oven at the middle level.

Season the cavity of the fish with lemon juice and salt and pepper. Rub one side of the fish with oil and season with salt and pepper.

Using oven mitts, remove the foil-lined rack from the oven, being careful to close the oven door, and set the rack down on the counter. Place the salmon, unseasoned side down, on the rack. Put the salmon in the oven and roast for 30 to 40 minutes. At the 30-minute mark, insert a thermometer into the thickest part—the fish is done if the thermometer registers 135°F.

Using a wide spatula, slide the salmon onto a warmed fish platter. Present the fish to your guests, then return to the kitchen to remove the skin and slice into individual portions. Pass the dressing at the table.

A variety of types of Christmas cards were widely available in Germany—where the tradition was established—decades earlier than in Britain or America. They are the design styles that lasted from the early 1840s into the first few decades of the twentieth century and are shown on pages 36 to 41. Especially prized were simple cards, beautifully printed or embossed, and intricate patterned die-cuts that were often three-dimensional. Decorative cards trimmed

with fringing, corded piping, and tassels. Cards detailed with areas that opened and closed or popped up or out when a cord was pulled were called transformation cards. All printed with a wide range of holiday images. The cards shown here were made between 1932 and 1937, and show a mix of old-fashioned Christmas images with contemporary patterns for their coordinating envelopes' fancy interiors—a later development that adds value to antique card collections.

Pirogi

4 medium baking potatoes, peeled

Sea salt

2 tablespoons unsalted butter

1 medium sweet onion, peeled and finely chopped

½ cup fine-curd cottage cheese, well drained

Freshly ground white pepper

Flour for dusting

25 to 30 egg roll wrappers (5¾-by- 6½-inches)

1 large egg, plus 1 teaspoon water, beaten together

Put the potatoes in a medium saucepan with enough water to cover, add a pinch of salt, and cover. Cook over medium-high heat for 25 to 45 minutes, until the potatoes show no resistance when pierced with a knife or fork. Remove from the heat and drain well.

While the potatoes are cooking, melt the butter in a small sauté pan or skillet and slowly cook the onions over low heat until translucent and soft. Do not let them brown.

With a potato ricer, mash the potatoes in a mixing bowl, and then add the onions and the cottage cheese. Continue mashing the mixture until all the ingredients are well blended and it is smooth. Season with salt and white pepper. Be sure the mashed potatoes are completely cool before proceeding to the next step.

Dust a marble surface or a plastic cutting board with flour, and arrange some of the egg roll wrappers on it. Put a rounded tablespoon of the potato filling on half of the wrapper, ⅜-inch from the edge. Brush the edges of the wrapper with the egg and water mixture, and gently fold the wrapper on the diagonal to form a triangle, then press down firmly along the edges to seal. Trim the pirogi to a half-moon shape using a sharp knife or the edge of a 4½-inch fluted pastry cutter. Set the pirogi on a platter and continue until all the filling and wrappers are used.

Bring a pot of salted water to a rapid boil over high heat. Reduce the heat to maintain a low boil and, working in batches and using a wide-slotted spatula, slide in the pirogi. Cook for 2 to 3 minutes. As they are done, transfer them to a warm platter or shallow serving bowl, and loosely cover with foil.

$\mathcal{A}$ whole fish will be needed to serve the number of dinner guests at the Christmas Eve feast, while the presentation of the salmon whole will be as impressive and festive as any traditional roasted holiday bird. To facilitate serving this large a group—and serving all the dishes hot—have the fish boned by the fishmonger, and pass the accompanying side dishes and sauce at the table, as you serve the salmon to each guest. Along with the pirogis, offer a bowl of leeks topped with some butter. The slow-cooking method used in this recipe for leek rounds keeps them flavorful and guarantees they will be so tender and soft they will melt in your mouth, while washing them once they've been sliced gets out all their bothersome grit. In addition offer some asparagus with fresh lemon squeezed over as a tasty garnish to the rest of the plate. (You will find the recipes for these vegetables on pages 156 and 157 in "The Pantry.")

A soapstone-topped antique French garden table serves instead of a traditional side board in my dining room. While fruit leaves and whole and sliced fruits decorate the silver serving platter for the salmon, an elegant arrangement of mixed foliage, white flowers and cabbages is displayed in a pitcher designed in the form of a nautilus shell with a mother-of-pearl finish and gilt handle. Like the pitcher, the fish servers are Victorian, but feature the classic dolphin motif for their decorative sea-themed design.

Light-as-a-Feather Cheesecake

———✦———

Many people may believe they have eaten the world's best cheesecake, but not if they haven't tasted one made with my sister-in-law Beatrice Oliver's recipe. It's so light and delicious I can only compare it to a glass of perfectly chilled champagne of the finest quality. It evaporates on the tongue. After a dinner of so many courses, it's just the right dessert. Here is her recipe, with one alteration: the crust she makes at home in England uses whole-meal digestive biscuits and ginger biscuits, for which I have substituted American cookies.

The cheesecake must be made the day before it is to be served as it needs to chill in the refrigerator overnight.

For the Crust

Vegetable oil

8 (3-inch) oatmeal cookies, broken into small pieces (about 5½ ounces)

9 (2-inch) gingersnaps (about 2 ounces)

6 tablespoons unsalted butter

For the Filling

½ cup sugar

¾ cup whole milk

Grated zest of 3 large lemons

1 rounded tablespoon unflavored gelatin powder

1 large egg yolk

Juice of 3 large lemons

¾ cup heavy cream

1 pound full-fat cottage cheese

3 large egg whites

¾ cup crème fraîche

The earliest Christmas presents would be put out around or on the tree branches without any packaging, while the paper cones or "cosques" that appeared later were decorated gift containers that hung on the tree. From the 1870s, a large business was done in novelty containers or fancy gift boxes made for the candy and chocolate trade and, to a lesser extent, the "Christmas cracker" industry. The decorative containers of papier-mâché or card stock were fashioned in the form of figures or objects—such as animals, Santa, his sleigh, or the yule log. The fanciest boxes were decorated with fabric or papers, ribbons, and printed scrap or greeting cards. Later, boxes and tins were printed with holiday motifs directly on their surface. Images of Santa, snowy villages, and characters from Victorian times are the most popular, even today.

MAKE THE CRUST: Lightly grease the inside of a 10-inch removable-bottom cake pan with oil.

Put the cookies and gingersnaps in the bowl of a food processor and process until they are fine crumbs.

Melt the butter over low heat, but do not let it brown. Remove from the heat, add the cookie crumbs, and stir until well blended.

Pour the mixture into the bottom of the cake pan, spreading it evenly and pressing down firmly to create a smooth flat base. Set aside.

MAKE THE FILLING: Put the sugar, milk, lemon zest, gelatin, and egg yolk in the bowl of a food processor, and process until it is thoroughly combined, 30 to 40 seconds. Pour the mixture into a small saucepan and cook over low heat, stirring constantly, until just heated through, about 3 minutes. Pour the contents of the saucepan back into the food processor, add the lemon juice and cream, and blend. While blending, spoon in the cottage cheese, and continue to process until the mixture is smooth, about 8 minutes.

Transfer the mixture to a large bowl, cover with plastic wrap, and refrigerate for 20 minutes. Remove the bowl from the refrigerator, stir the mixture, and refrigerate for another 10 minutes. Remove from the refrigerator and check to see if the mixture is thickening and has become syrupy. If it isn't, return the bowl to the refrigerator and check again after 5 minutes. When the liquid is syrupy and about to set, transfer to the food processor and blend until smooth and silky, about 30 seconds. Return the mixture to the chilled bowl and set aside.

In another bowl, using an electric hand mixer, whisk the egg whites until they form soft peaks. With a metal spoon, fold half of the egg whites into the cheese mixture, then fold in the remaining egg whites. Gently stir in the crème fraîche.

Pour the filling into the prepared crust, cover with foil, and refrigerate overnight.

To unmold the cheesecake, rinse a clean tea towel in hot running water, squeeze out the excess water, and wrap the towel around the sides of the pan for 5 seconds.

Holding the side of the cake pan with one hand, push up on the bottom and ease the cheesecake onto a serving plate. Serve immediately or refrigerate.

Accompany with fresh mixed berries—such as blueberries, raspberries, and strawberries sprinkled over with some sugar.

Christmas Day Lunch

SERVES 8 TO 10

HORS D'OEUVRES
"Chips" and Dips

Pâté Stuffed Mushroom Caps

•

STARTERS
Individual Truffle-Scented Cheese Soufflés

Macaroni and Cheese

BOUZY ROUGE

•

MAIN COURSE
Deep-Fried Turkey

•

SIDES
Wild Rice and Risotto Jambalaya Dressing

Baked Winter Vegetables

Spicy Cranberry Sauce and Maple-Walnut Cranberry Sauce

CÔTES DE BLAYE

•

DESSERT
Bûche de Noël

SPARKLING SHIRAZ

Good tidings we bring to you and your kin . . . .
We wish you a Merry Christmas and a happy New Year

SINCE I WAS A CHILD, I HAVE LOOKED FORWARD TO Christmas day with eager anticipation. Although the word *glorious* was quite a mouthful for me then, it was most appropriate. The word captures the magical sights and sounds of the day: the sparkle and shine of a world made bright by lights, tinsel, and smiles, and the joyful music that rings out over the cold, crisp air from pealing church bells, choir voices, and happy laughter in the home.

Whenever my parents hosted the family Christmas, the aroma wafting from the turkey cooking in the oven would fill our home for hours, and whet our appetites for the meal that would be shared later with my grandmother, aunts, uncles, and cousins. We celebrated at midday, ostensibly to avoid late drives home and kids kept up too long past bedtime. However, I remember that in the evening an impromptu supper would hastily be put together from the leftovers of the first meal, and children were often carried out to the car for the journey home, fast asleep.

When I took over as host, I carried on the tradition of a holiday lunch. So, like my mother and my aunts, I never get to use all those recipes that appear in magazines with inventive dishes created from holiday table's leftovers. The most I can do is a stock from the turkey's carcass.

MENU: The dishes center around the traditional holiday bird—turkey—with its dressing and cranberry sauce. As this is a family meal there is something to please children and adults alike from start to finish. Hence the chips with dips and the pâté-filled mushrooms, the macaroni and cheese casserole and the truffle-scented cheese soufflés, the simple mixed vegetables (which can be picked at for preferred bits) and the spicy jambalya dressing. The Bûche pleases guests of all ages and stands out as a most decorative dessert, representing the ancient yule log in an edible form.

TABLE AND DECORATIONS: This is Christmas at our house. I love the outdoors and the old-fashioned, so my choice of decorations has been relatively consistent over the years. Objects from nature are transformed into decorations, and the types of ornaments that were found on the earliest Christmas trees are used as well.

A big tree and plenty of fresh evergreens, in vases and pots and as wreaths and garlands, are placed all through the house—the smell of pine permeates the air. Pinecones I've collected on country walks in England and Scotland, and gather now from the forest around our home here are used for decorations, as are sand dollar shells that were collected from the beaches near my parents' and brother's Florida homes. Bright red accents in the form of tartan ribbons, shiny balls and apple ornaments, cardinals, candles, and bouquets of roses are everywhere.

TRADITIONS: *M*any of the evergreens used inside and outside the home at Christmas were originally used as protection against evil and offerings to the gods. Their use by ancient Egyptians, Chinese, Hebrews, Greeks, and Romans is well known, but there are links to even earlier peoples. Boughs, wreaths, garlands, and swags have been symbolically displayed in civic and religious places and homes for millennia.

The significance of the yule log can be traced back to the early pagan festival of the Winter Solstice. A tree was cut down and its trunk brought home to provide a long, slow-burning fire that would give warmth and light during the weeklong December holiday. Many superstitions attributed magical powers to its unburned core or its ashes. Over time, decorative replica logs made of materials such as plaster of Paris, or ornamental log-shaped boxes made of card or papier-mâché replaced the actual log in traditions. Eventually, the log evolved into the Christmas dessert we know today—a cake re-creating the log in detail. As with its earlier versions, a toy robin often sits perched on the yule log cake.

The association of the robin with the log comes to us from the Middle Ages and is based on the myth that the bird brought the first fire to earth; singeing his feathers, he acquired his distinctive red breast. Another legend attributes this coloring to a wound made by a thorn from Christ's crown, which is why the robin is also frequently depicted with holly, the shrub from which the crown was said to have been made.

The Christmas tree and its ornaments derive from two German traditions, the Paradise tree and Christmas pyramid. The Paradise tree originated as part of the "stage set" for a medieval mystery play about Adam and Eve frequently performed around December 24—their feast day. It was a fir hung with apples and surrounded by candles, representing the Garden of Eden. Over time, the tree found its way into the home, and wafers symbolizing the Eucharist were added as Christmas decorations—later decorative cookies took their place. The Christmas pyramid was a triangular construction that could be crudely fashioned from twigs or more elaborately built as tiered wooden shelves that could hold Christmas figures, as well as evergreens, candles, and a star.

From the sixteenth century, the types of ornaments for the tree drew from both these sources. The Christmas tree arrived in America with the early German settlers of the seventeenth century. It had become immensely popular here and in most of Europe by the nineteenth century. The widespread success of the decorated tree is often attributed to the faithful observance of the custom by Queen Victoria and her German-born husband, Prince Albert. In the latter part of the nineteenth century and early part of the twentieth century the tree tradition had even found its way to China and Japan by way of American missionaries.

The Christmas cracker evolved from a mid-nineteenth-century street custom not unlike the use of fire-crackers around the Fourth of July: children tossed small balls that exploded in the streets as noisemakers. The explosive balls were quickly replaced with crackers, the cardboard tubes filled with treats that we are familiar with today, and were part of festive table decorations from Victorian times. Crackers usually came as boxed sets, and held a nosiy snapper and little favors, but the degree to which the containers and the crackers were artfully designed and ornately trimmed, as well as the quantity and quality of the treats within, varied greatly according to price. Crackers were snapped and then opened at the table, their treasure spilling out to the joy of the merrymakers.

COLLECTIBLES: *C*hristmas evergreens are a perennial decorative theme, surviving from earlier times as printed images, trade and greeting cards, ornamental boxes or tins, and prints.

Some gift boxes, candy containers, and miniature table decorations representing the yule log with a robin perched atop survive from Victorian times and the early years of the twentieth century. The robin was also popular as a clip-on tree ornament and in printed images of evergreens and winter scenes.

Christmas crackers are highly treasured by collectors. Widely produced as they were, intact, unopened ones are hard to come by since they would have been "consumed" during the festivities, and are hence quite valuable. A set of crackers in a lace-trimmed cardboard box, wrapped in fancy tissue, might hold tiny toys, charms, or cheap jewels. Others created as special editions or commissioned sets might use a silver box as a container and feature real gold and silver jewelry, and would be valued for the containers and contents. Complete sets in their original packaging are rare finds.

Since the days when we lived in England, our holiday table is never without Christmas crackers (opposite). They become part of the table's decoration, as well as part of the festivities.Christmas guests arriving from London never turn up without a set.
Certainly of greater value are antique crackers, like these rare finds from different sets displayed in an 1850s bowl, part of my blue and white collection.

Pâté Stuffed Mushroom Caps

---

30 small cremini mushrooms (about ¾- to 1-inch diameter),
    cleaned, stems cut off, and scooped out

Sea salt

Freshly ground black pepper

6 ounces good-quality pâté

Heat a large nonstick wok or sauté pan over medium-high heat until very hot.
Add the mushroom caps and cook, stirring constantly, for 5 to 6 minutes, until
they are tender but firm and give when pressed with the back of a spoon. Transfer
the mushrooms to a bowl lined with paper towels, cover with a paper towel, and
keep them warm.

Pat the mushrooms dry with some paper towels, season with salt and pepper,
and spoon ½ teaspoon of the pâté into each cap. Serve immediately.

Hors d'Oeuvres: With the advent of
"gourmet" chips and dips, you can purchase
interesting and tasty nibbles to serve without
shame. Potato chips now come in a choice of
tantalizing flavors, while the chips themselves
come from a variety of types of potatoes and
other flavorful root vegetables—such as yam,
sweet potato, beet, or turnip. Good quality
dips of puréed or chopped vegetables are
widely available—such as hummus and
salsa. Offer a choice, but don't forget the
"plain kind" of chips for the kids!

*Christmas just isn't Christmas without the tree.
It is the center of the holiday's activities—
the day for decorating it, the night for lighting it,
the morning opening presents around it. A thing
of great beauty, it stands proudly with its lights
burning bright throughout the long festive season.
While the earliest trees to be brought into
the home as part of a winter ritual may have been
the date palms that marked the Winter Solstice
for the ancient Egyptians or the candlelit trees
that marked Saturnalia for the Romans, the
decorated trees that most resemble today's were
the Paradise tree and the Christmas pyramids of
Germany—the former dating from the Middle
Ages. A charming legend has it that the first
decorated tree originated at the first Christmas.
All God's creatures—including trees—had
gathered in Bethlehem to bring the Christ Child
a gift. While some trees could offer their blossoms
or fruits, the fir tree had only its evergreen leaves.
An angel took pity and scattered stars from the
sky over the fir tree's branches. The infant was
thrilled to see the shining tree and blessed it, and
the custom of the decorated evergreen was born.
The family decorated tree became a holiday
"household" item by the nineteenth century,
and civic trees (those mounted in public places)
became, over time, a custom as well.*

Individual Truffle-Scented Cheese Soufflés

For the soufflé you'll need 10 individual 7½-ounce ramekins. If you cannot find the Italian black-truffle-flavored sheep's milk cheese substitute Gruyère and use Parmesan cheese to dust ramekins, and you might also purchase a truffle to pass with a small cheese grater at the table (see page 163 for sources of cheese).

6 tablespoons unsalted butter, plus additional for the ramekins

6 tablespoons finely grated plain hard sheep's milk cheese

2 cups whole milk

6 tablespoons flour

Sea salt

Pinch of cayenne

Pinch of ground nutmeg

8 large eggs, separated, plus 1 egg white

Freshly ground black pepper

7 ounces finely grated sottocenere al tartu (truffle cheese)

Preheat the oven to 400°F, setting the rack at the middle level.

Butter the ramekins, then sprinkle them with the plain sheep's milk cheese (as you would dust a baking dish with flour). Wrap 14-by-4-inch sheets of greaseproof paper around each ramekin and tie with kitchen string to secure. Set aside.

Put the milk in a small saucepan and bring to a boil. While the milk is coming to a boil, melt 6 tablespoons butter in another saucepan over low heat, add the flour, and cook, stirring with a wooden spoon, until it foams, about 2 minutes. Remove the pan from the heat. When the mixture stops foaming, vigorously whisk in the boiling milk, and continue to whisk until the mixture is smooth and creamy.

Place over medium-high heat, add 1 teaspoon salt, the cayenne, and nutmeg, and whisk. Cook, continuing to whisk, until the mixture resembles a heavy, thick cream, about 1 minute. Immediately remove the pan from the heat.

The first ornaments for the tree were edible—fruits, nuts, cookies and other sweet treats were suspended from its branches. Later, cone-shaped packets and tiny gift boxes containing sweets and small toys were also used and taken from the tree to be "consumed." Imitations of these real-life treats and gifts were later manufactured as ornaments and became quite common after 1860. But a complete list of the variety of materials and designs of ornaments that were used and created over time is seemingly endless.

Miniature musical instruments—an ever popular motif—are linked to the toy drums and horns that might be given to children for Christmas. As the German factories that produced toys were the first into the Christmas market, other toys were adapted as ornaments too. The nutcracker was a popular child's toy, made to resemble an ugly little man, it had a grotesque jaw, which could be opened to crack nuts. Decked out in a soldier's fancy dress uniform, it was the embodiment of the character made familiar to children in E.T.A. Hoffman's

tale "The Nutcracker and the Mouse King" and famous by Tchaikovsky's ballet. A witch's curse turns a handsome prince into the ugly nutcracker, but a battle against an army of mighty mice returns him to human form.

Glass ornaments in the form of birds, with their rainbow plummage and spun glass tails, are a perennial delight with their clip-on fixtures that allow them to perch on and seemingly dart among the tree's branches to charming effect.

Drop one egg yolk into the center of the mixture and whisk to blend thoroughly. Repeat with remaining egg yolks, adding them one at a time and incorporating each one before adding the next. Set aside.

Put the egg whites in a large bowl, add a pinch of salt, and whisk until soft peaks form. With a metal spoon slowly fold one-quarter of the whisked egg whites into the yolk mixture. Then fold in 6 ounces of the *sottocenere al tartu* cheese. Fold in the remaining whisked egg whites.

Divide the mixture equally among the prepared ramekins and gently tap them on the counter to ensure that the mixture is evenly distributed. Sprinkle the remaining 1 ounce *sottocenere al tartu* cheese over the ramekins.

Bake for 20 to 30 minutes, until the soufflés have puffed up. (Do not open the oven while they are baking, or they will collapse or not rise.)

When the soufflés are done, remove them from the oven, carefully remove the paper wraps, and serve immediately.

Deep-Fried Turkey

———※———

A long time ago, while I was still living in England, I received the traditional gift of a Christmas turkey from a company with which I regularly did business. It was a very large turkey! So large, in fact, that it didn't fit in my oven. My husband, Michel, saved the day by grilling the big bird in our Weber kettle barbecue. From that day forward, no turkey of ours saw the inside of an oven—we preferred to grill it. That is, until Michel purchased a deep-fat frying kettle last year. Deep frying produces a wonderfully succulent bird, not greasy in the least, and the cooking process is so very quick. The only drawbacks are that the standard fryer available from many stores accommodates a turkey no larger than 18 pounds and you can't stuff the turkey.

I strongly recommend brining the turkey for a few hours and then marinating it overnight to flavor the bird. Submerging it in oil will eliminate any herb or spice coatings, and loosening the skin to place seasoning underneath may cause the skin to pull back during frying. Should you decide to roast your bird this year in the traditional way, the brining and this marinade can still be used as preparation.

Because the oil goes into the fryer first and is heated to a high temperature, you need to figure out exactly how much oil you'll need in advance—before the turkey is submerged in the hot oil. Oil will be displaced by the bird, and if there is too much oil in the fryer to begin with, it will overflow. After unwrapping the turkey and emptying the cavity, place the bird in the fryer and pour water in over it to the measuring mark on the fryer. Remove the turkey and note the water level in the fryer. When it's time to fry the turkey, pour in oil just to that level. You can also pour the water from the fryer into a container to accurately measure the quantity used. Either method should eliminate the possibility of dangerous spills. Be sure the turkey is completely thawed if you're using a frozen bird, and pat the turkey dry before putting it into the hot oil.

The Children's Table: It's a long-standing family tradition to set a separate table for the young ones when guests are numerous and the time spent at the table will be leisurely by adult standards—and overly long by children's. On Christmas, it's an especially welcome arrangement for parents and kids alike. The excitement of the day has the youngest children as over energized as the bunny in the battery ad, which can tax even the most patient adult. Creating a setting and table with a decorative theme that is special and festive but made just for the children, will delight them and keep them amused. In planning the food, it's wise to keep the preferences of young palates in mind, and offer some dishes they regard as treats. This menu offers a very special soufflé made with a truffle-perfumed cheese that most kids would shy away from, so a kid-pleasing dish of macaroni and cheese is recommended for their starter (see recipe on page 159).

A perennial favorite frequently found under the Christmas tree, teddy bears placed around their holiday table will create equal delight for the children. They were named for the American president Theodore Roosevelt because he was said to have saved a bear cub's life. Since then, bears have been objects of great affection for young and old alike.

For the Turkey

1 (15- to 18-pound) free-range turkey, free of hormone additives
and antibiotics, cavity emptied, rinsed

8 cups kosher salt or coarse sea salt

For the Marinade

¾ cup coarsely chopped thyme

½ cup coarsely chopped sage

2 tablespoons freshly cracked black peppercorns

1 tablespoon sea salt

3 large cloves garlic, crushed

2 cups extra-virgin olive oil

Vegetable oil for frying (see headnote)

Place the turkey in a large clean plastic bucket or scrubbed-down work sink and add water to cover completely. Pour in the salt and leave in a cool place for 2 to 3 hours. Remove from the brining bath and rinse thoroughly inside and out. Pat dry with paper towels.

MAKE THE MARINADE: Combine the thyme, sage, pepper, salt, garlic, and olive oil in a large measuring cup and stir to mix. Set aside.

When the brining is finished, place three large kitchen trash bags inside one another and set the triple-layered bags on a large platter. Roll down the sides and place the turkey in the bags. Stir the marinade and then pour over the turkey. Pull up the sides of the bags slightly and baste the bird with the marinade. Draw up the bags to completely enclose the turkey, press the air out, and tie the top securely. Place in the refrigerator on one side. During the evening before cooking, turn the bird once or twice and leave it breast side up overnight. The next morning, remove the turkey from the refrigerator and let it come to room temperature before cooking.

COOK THE TURKEY: Soak a few bamboo skewers in water for 30 minutes.

Heat the vegetable oil in the deep-fat fryer.

Untie the marinating bags and roll down the sides. Transfer the turkey onto the spit of the fryer. Close the cavity with some of the skewers, and trim with shears if necessary. Tie the legs together with kitchen twine. When the oil has reached the required temperature, gently lower the bird, on the spit, into the oil. Cover and cook for 3½ minutes per pound.

Remove the turkey from the fryer and take it off the spit. Place it on a large carving board and let it rest in a warm place, loosely covered with foil, for 20 to 30 minutes. Carve and place the turkey slices on a platter or onto individual plates.

Wild Rice and Risotto Jambalaya Dressing

This dressing is prepared on the stove top and then cooked in the oven in a baking dish; it is not stuffed in the turkey.

Sea salt

3 tablespoons extra-virgin olive oil

1 pound andouille sausage (or other Cajun-style or spicy smoked sausage), thinly sliced

1 onion, finely chopped

3 cloves garlic, finely chopped

2 stalks celery, diced (½ cup)

1½ sweet red peppers, cored, seeded, and diced (2 cups)

2 teaspoons dried thyme, crumbled

2 bay leaves

½ teaspoon freshly ground black pepper

⅛ to ¼ teaspoon cayenne pepper (optional)

½ teaspoon filé powder

1 recipe Cooked Wild Rice, about 1½ cups (see page 157)

1 recipe Cooked Himalayan Red Rice, about 1½ cups (see page 157)

1 recipe Basic Risotto, about 3 cups (see page 158)

1 cup canned chopped tomatoes, drained

3 or 4 scallions, thinly sliced (½ cup)

1 pound lump crabmeat, picked over for shells and broken up with a fork

Preheat the oven to 350°F.

Heat the oil in a sauté pan over medium heat. Add the sausage and cook until golden brown and just about to turn crisp, about 10 minutes. Remove from the heat and, using a slotted spoon, transfer the sausage to a bowl.

Return the pan to the heat and add the onion, garlic, celery, red peppers, thyme, bay leaves, 1 teaspoon salt, black pepper, cayenne, and filé powder to the pan and

stir to mix well. Cover and cook over low heat until the vegetables are tender, stirring occasionally, 12 to 15 minutes. Transfer to a bowl and set aside.

Combine the cooked rices and risotto in a large bowl. Stir in the sausage, cooked vegetables, and the tomatoes, scallions, and crabmeat. Transfer the dressing to a 10½-by-14-by-2-inch porcelain or glass baking dish and cover loosely with foil. Bake for 15 minutes, remove the foil and bake for another 10 minutes, until heated through.

Baked Winter Vegetables

—❧❦—

*T*he beets and Brussels sprouts are precooked—they may be prepared as early as the night before—and at room temperature when added. To cut the eight circles of butternut squash, choose one with a long neck of 4- to 5-inch diameter.

Beets

> 10 baby or small beets (about 1¾-inch diameter) scrubbed,
>   stems trimmed to 1½ inches and root end to ½ inch, and halved

Preheat the oven to 400°F, setting the rack at the middle level.

Arrange the beets in a baking dish, cut side up. Pour in water to come about ¼-inch up the sides. Loosely cover with foil and bake until tender, 50 minutes.

Drain and set aside.

Brussels sprouts

> Sea salt
>
> 1 to 1¼ pounds Brussels sprouts (about 20 to 24), root end trimmed
>   and cut with an "X" ⅛-inch deep, exterior and damaged leaves removed

Bring a saucepan of salted water to a boil and add the Brussels sprouts. Cook until tender, about 8 to 10 minutes from the time the water comes back to a boil.

Drain and rinse under cold water. Set aside while you prepare the squash and onions (see following page).

Squash and Onions

   2 tablespoons plus 2 teaspoons balsamic vinegar, plus additional

   1 tablespoon plus 1 teaspoon finely chopped thyme

   ½ cup extra-virgin olive oil

   4 teaspoons kosher salt or coarse sea salt, plus additional

   8 (½-inch) round slices peeled butternut squash, 8 wedges cut
      from each slice

   5 or 6 small onions (about 2 inches diameter), peeled and
      quartered

Preheat the oven to 375°F, setting the rack at the middle level.

Combine the vinegar and thyme in a measuring cup and slowly whisk in the oil.

Pour ⅔ of the oil mixture into a large mixing bowl with 3 teaspoons of the salt, and add the squash wedges and the onions. Transfer the vegetables to a foil-lined pan. Add half of the remaining oil mixture to the mixing bowl with 1 teaspoon of the salt. Toss to coat.

Loosely cover with foil and bake for 40 to 50 minutes, until just tender. Stir every 15 minutes.

Meanwhile, toss the cooked Brussels sprouts in some of the remaining oil mixture and salt. Sprinkle some vinegar and salt over the cooked beets. Add the beets and sprouts to the onions in the pan and cook for another 15 minutes. Transfer the vegetables to a warm serving dish.

Bûche de Noël

The tradition of dressing an evergreen tree with beautiful ornaments for Christmas was not just a family affair by the second half of the nineteenth century, and as depicted in the charming German chromolith from 1875 (seen opposite). An entire industry rose up around this Christmas ritual—first in Germany, later in America, and lastly in Japan. Companies were formed for the manufacture of lights, ornaments, tree blankets, and stands for the tree. By the twentieth century, Christmas—including seasonal greeting cards and wrappings—had grown into the big business it is today. And Christmas antiques are not just sentimental family heirlooms—as this chromolith also shows, it could be worth a few hundred dollars.

The history of many of these decorations and the tree are noted like landmark events—a list of these facts make fascinating reading if not a wonderful Christmas parlor game. Here's a small sampling just for fun: The sale of the first commercial glass ornaments is noted in 1848; tinsel's invented in 1878 and materials are refined in the 1920s and 60s; the first White House tree is set up in 1856; the feather tree appears in the 1860s; Christmas is finally a legal holiday in all of the United States in 1890; ornament hooks appear in 1892; the first White House tree to use electric lights is switched on in 1895; tree lights for the home are made by G.E. in 1901, strings of lights by Ever-Ready in 1903, lights wired in series in 1907; "The Shiny Brite" ornament company is founded in the late 1930s; clear glass ornaments painted with stripes are made in the 1940s due to rationing of materials during WWII . . . and there's much more!

There are many variations of the yule log cake's recipe and even more for its decoration. This is my sister-in-law's version, which produces a holiday treat that's both delicious and beautiful as a centerpiece for the dessert table. It is made of a light sponge base, then filled and iced with a chocolate buttercream flavored with a hint of bourbon.

Note: The cake can be completed a few hours before serving.

For the sponge base:

6 eggs

¾ cups granulated sugar, plus additional for the pan

1 cup all-purpose flour, sifted

6 tablespoons unsalted butter, melted in a double boiler, plus additional unmelted for the pan

For the filling and icing:

5 ounces sweetened dark chocolate (for baking or eating)

4 ounces lump sugar (cubes)

5 egg yolks

8 tablespoons unsalted butter, cut into small bits

1 tablespoon bourbon

½ teaspoon vanilla extract

MAKE THE SPONGE BASE: Preheat the oven to 350°F, setting the rack at the middle level.

In a large heat-resistant bowl, combine the eggs and sugar and whisk until blended.

Set the bowl over a pan of simmering water—the bowl should not touch the water. Using a wire whisk or an electric hand mixer, beat until the mixture is just warm, 5 to 10 minutes.

With the bowl still sitting on top of the pan, carefully remove from the heat and whisk until the mixture has tripled in volume, about 20 minutes by hand or 10 with

(continued)

an electric mixer. Take the bowl off the pan, and with a metal spoon gently fold in the flour until well incorporated, then add a third of the butter. Repeat the process, alternating the flour and the butter, until all has been used.

Butter a 9-by-12-inch jelly roll pan, dust with flour, and line the bottom with greaseproof paper.

Pour the batter into the pan and bake for 35 to 40 minutes, until the sponge has risen, is springy to the touch, and has detached from the sides of the pan. A knife point or toothpick will come out clean when inserted in the center. Let the sponge cool for about 5 minutes, then turn it out onto a clean tea towel topped with a lightly sugared sheet of greaseproof paper. Remove the paper from the top of the sponge and trim off any crusty edges if necessary. On the short sides of the sponge, cut 3 slits 1-inch long from the outer edge toward the center. Cover the sponge with another sheet of greaseproof paper. Pick up the short ends of the tea towel underneath the sponge and roll up the sponge around the paper. Immediately cover the roll with a lightly dampened tea towel and set aside. The cake should be completely cooled before icing and assembling.

MAKE THE FILLING AND ICING: Place the chocolate in a heat-resistant bowl and set it over a saucepan of simmering water—the bowl should not touch the water.

Slowly melt the chocolate over low heat.

While the chocolate is melting, add the sugar to a saucepan with 7 tablespoons of water and cook until the sugar melts, stirring constantly. Set a candy or preserve thermometer in the pan, increase the heat, and bring to a boil. When the temperature reaches 215°F or the consistency of the liquid appears as small threads, about 20 seconds, remove the pan from the heat and set the syrup aside.

In a bowl and using a wire whisk or an electric hand mixer, beat the egg yolks until they are a thick and creamy consistency, about 5 minutes. In a steady stream, beating constantly, slowly pour in the syrup; beat until the volume of the bowl's contents has doubled, and has cooled, about 15 minutes.

In another bowl, mash the butter to a smooth cream using a wooden spoon, about 10 minutes. Pour the sugar and egg mixture in a slow, steady stream, stirring constantly, until all the ingredients have been well incorporated. The butter cream will be smooth, firm, and shiny.

Stir in the bourbon until well blended. Put 3½ ounces of this mixture into a small bowl and stir in the vanilla. Set aside.

Add the melted chocolate to the large bowl of butter cream and blend thoroughly. Refrigerate for 15 minutes.

*L*ike many, I am an ardent lover of blue and white pottery. I'm drawn to it whether old or new and no matter which process produced the beautiful designs nor for what purpose the pieces were created. Few pieces, if any, of my collection are too precious to make use of every day, let alone use for special occasions—but I treasure them all. And the historical importance of blue and white patterned pottery bears out my approach in collecting.

Transferware refers to the process of transferring a design from a copperplate to paper and then onto pottery. The technique proved most successful when applied to unglazed pottery that was later fired as the results were long lasting. Blue was used, as cobalt was the color that could take the high heat of firing. Flow blue was created by allowing the design to bleed during firing. Underglaze printing and the development of ironstone china as a substitute for porcelain in the early nineteenth century at Staffordshire, England, were important in making decorative tableware in complete services and other pottery objects available to the middle class, as they could be cheaply and mass produced.

Assemble and decorate the bûche: The butter creams are difficult to work with when too warm. You will find it helpful to refrigerate both the log and the butter cream from time to time while you are assembling the bûche. Ice and decorate the cake on a base you will use when serving, as once decorated you will not want to move it.

Unroll the sponge and remove the greaseproof paper. Sprinkle with some additional bourbon if you wish. Using the chocolate butter cream, spread some over the top of the sponge to completely cover the surface with ⅛-inch thickness of the butter cream. Carefully roll up the sponge from one of its short sides. Turn the roll so that the seam is at the bottom. Transfer to a flat cake base that will be suitable for serving.

Now spread the circle ends of the roll with the bourbon-flavored butter cream. Create a "tree knot" for the log with a mound of the buttercream, placing it off center and on an angle toward one end of the roll.

Using an icing bag with a star-shaped #30 nozzle, pipe chocolate butter cream in rows down the length of the log until completely covered to look like bark on a log.

Change to a plain #2 nozzle, and pipe a few concentric circles of chocolate icing at each end to imitate the rings of the tree. Refrigerate for 30 minutes or until the icing is firm.

Using a sharp knife with a warmed blade, slice through the "tree knot" on an angle parallel to the surface of the log, to create the appearance of a sawn-off tree branch.

Decorate the bûche with some Christmas greens, fresh cranberries, and a Christmas robin, and surround the log with more greens. Sprinkle some confectioners' sugar over the cake and the serving plate to create a snowy effect.

Serve a slice of cake to each guest on its own, or with a scoop of ice cream on the side.

White Christmas Dinner

SERVES 10

HORS D'OEUVRES
Prosciutto-Wrapped Prunes
Assorted Olives, Nuts, and Cheese Sticks

CHINON

•

STARTER
Crabmeat Ravioli

VIOGNIER

•

MAIN COURSE
Prime Rib Roast

•

SIDES
Yorkshire Pudding
Whipped Creamed Horseradish Sauce
Creamed Baby Spinach and Watercress

RIOJA

•

DESSERT
Chocolate Mousse with Fresh Raspberries

BEAUMES DE VENISE

Dashing through the snow,
in a one-horse open sleigh . . .

EVERYONE WOULD HAVE TO AGREE THAT THE PERFECT Christmas is a snowy white one, just as in many songs we know and love so well. Too often, though, it is only a dream, as Christmas snowfalls are rare in many areas. But I don't let that stop me from creating a shimmering and sparkling white setting for a special holiday celebration.

While I do stop short of hiring snow-making machines and spraying cans of foamy white stuff all around the house, I have been known to sprinkle a bit of fake snowflakes here and there. But the simplest approach is a focus on snow-white hues and frosty silver shades for the table setting and the decorative objects around the house to create a winter wonderland effect.

Although we favor a lunch as the special meal at Christmas, an evening celebration is preferred by many. A nighttime setting automatically creates an elegant and even romantic ambiance, which can be greatly enhanced by the flickering light of a fire and candles.

MENU: *A*long with a turkey or goose, a roast of beef is a very traditional main course for a Christmas celebration. As so many of us today limit our intake of red meat in our regular diets, serving a roasted beef dish will be very special indeed. A prime rib roast ensures that the finest cut of meat will be served to all, and will make a dish look as impressive as it is tasty. Here, it teams up with its classic accompaniments of Yorkshire pudding and a creamy horseradish sauce that's whipped to fluffy perfection. In our home, the traditional partner for beef dinners is spinach—we love it pureed with watercress and cream. A few prunes wrapped in prosciutto, some cheese sticks, and a selection of flavorful olives and nuts offered with "cocktails" won't be too much before this rich meal. The crabmeat-filled "raviolis" offer a complete contrast of taste between the hors d'oeuvres and main course. After a filling dinner such as this one, the dessert must be utterly irresistible. As basic as this creamy mousse may be, I've never known anyone to pass up some-

thing with chocolate. Spoon out the mousse with some forgiving raspberries to balance the rich with the righteous.

Table and Decorations: *A*ll year round, collections of antique white ironstone plates and pottery, mercury glass candlesticks, vases, urns, and silver napkin rings are the design feature of the interior of this home. At Christmas, they provide the basis for creating a dreamy winter wonderland effect with their snowy color and frosty shimmer. Especially appropriate for the holiday look are the silver-sprayed wreaths and dried leaves, fruits, nuts, and vegetables and the collection of antique snowmen and snow character figures. At dinner, dozens of candles burn brightly, their effect doubled in the dining room mirror and their light reflected in the display of silvery objects on the table. The everyday basic white stoneware plates are as luminous as the best fine porcelain china in the glow of so much candlelight.

Traditions: *W*reaths are considered circular garlands, while festoons and swags are draped garlands. The use of garlands for decoration in homes and religious or civic places has a long history—flowers and fruits as well as green foliage were traditionally used. The first wreaths associated with Christmas would be the Advent Wreath that became part of the ritual of the monthlong holy period leading up to

Christmas Day. Made into a small-sized table wreath from a fir garland, it was ornamented with five candles which would be lit one at a time on each of the four Sundays of Advent and the fifth on Christmas Day— the ritual lighting would be accompanied by the reading of scripture and prayer. In the nineteenth century, evergreen wreaths were popular, made with decorative accents of pinecones, nuts and holly with its festive red berries. Today, the holiday wreaths that are hung on doors, over mantelpieces, in windows, and laid out on tables are often highly decorated and as ornamental as the Christmas tree itself.

While the origin of the snowman can be generally attributed to natural events and some artistic ingenuity on the part of those engaged in winter outdoor play activities, many snow characters developed as part of decorations designed for the tree, miniature Christmas villages, or the festive holiday table—and particularly to top the special Christmas dessert. Santa's elves, infants or toddlers bundled up in snowsuits, snowmen, polar bears, teddys, and other animals were some of the most popular characters that could be found atop a snow-white iced Christmas cake or within a snow scene arrangement for the table. These charming figures were represented dressed for polar climes and often engaged in holiday or arctic pursuits, such as caroling, bringing home the tree, skiing, sledding, skating, or playing in the snow. They were colored in white and made of bisque, porcelain, or composition. Their garments were given a furry effect with a textured finish, which was created by applying grog to the bisque before the piece was fired. Often, figures were made of a mixture of materials. Of the snow figures, those specifically of the tiny tots became extremely popular in the first decade of the twentieth century and are appropriately called snow babies. However, the term is often used to include other characters with the same furry finish. The kiddie snow babies are still manufactured today, as are the ever popular snowman figures. Snowmen were characteristically made up of round ball bodies and heads imitating those made from rolling up snow in your backyard, but often plump arms and even chubby legs were added as creative invention. And just like the outdoor originals, miniature snowmen were frequently accessorized with a hat, scarf, and a switch or broom, while their signature face was made with bits of coal. In antique form, snowmen were made in an even greater variety of materials than the other snow characters, including wax, glass, papier-mâché, and wood. His image, as well as the activity of making a snowman, was a popular theme for Victorian greeting and trade cards and occasionally winter scenic oil paintings. With his round ample shape, he was a particularly popular character for candy containers, as he could be filled with lots of treats. As the subject of many children's books and, of course, that famous song about Frosty, the snowman is a beloved snow character. Today's figures are produced in decorative three-dimensional forms for the tree or table, and as toys or as printed images on everything from seasonal greeting cards and gift wrappings to household linens for the kitchen, dining table, and even bedroom. And snowmen still appear in yards after a good snowfall.

COLLECTIBLES: *The* general category of miniature snow figures, and specifically that of snow babies, is a focus of collectors of old and new Christmas objects. The immense popularity of special decorations for the Christmas cake meant that a great quantity were produced and widely distributed by department stores and early specialty chains and were also readily available from local shops—their sheer numbers ensured that many survive today. And as the figures themselves were designed in such an extensive variety of types, a collection of snow babies can exhibit an interesting diversity—a most desirable quality. Snow babies date from the first decades of the twentieth century, while other snow figures were made earlier—snowmen as early as the 1870s.

The three delightful snow figures on the opposite page are quite typical of the design and mix of materials used in the early decades of the twentieth century and would have been perfect fixtures for the Christmas table or snow village arrangement. The snow baby at left is of modern production, but in the style of the first furry finished antiques. For the collector of modern snow babies, they are equally as charming in their design as the early ones.

In an all-white dining room, a white painted table is laid with place settings of plain white ironstone and linen napkins, creating a snowy background for the frosty shimmer and shine of silvery decorations. More than a dozen of creamy white candles—their number and effect doubled in the large framed mirror's reflection—create a dreamy glow. The flickering light from the candles dances on the surface of an abundance of silver finished objects used to dress the holiday table. Tree ornaments attached to silver gift tags are draped over each napkin to serve as place cards, while others are scattered around to offset the silver goblets and part of a collection of antique mercury glass that is used for the centerpiece down the length of the table. More of the glass is set out over the fireplace below a wreath of sprayed silver leaves, carrying the winter wonderland theme into the living room (pages 74–75).

   Although referred to as mercury glass and sometimes silvered glass, these pieces contain neither mercury nor silver. Produced from the early nineteenth century as a molded blown glass made of double-walled clear glass—the "silver" (and later other colors) was introduced between the two layers of glass through a small hole in the object that was then closed with a plug. It was produced plain and also patterned—designs were painted on, or were etched with acid or by cutting. Candlesticks and doorknobs were almost exclusively the first objects made, vases became popular later. Around 1900, the glass was fashionable as Christmas ornaments.

Crabmeat Ravioli

———❦———

I serve three of these "ravioli" in a fish or miso broth when the dish is meant as a more substantial starter. However, in the context of this menu, a simple lime and garlic–flavored dressing to drizzle over the ravioli is all that is needed. Serve 1, 2 or 3 ravioli per person and according to appetites.

You may need to double the egg wash.

For the Dressing

¾ cup extra-virgin olive oil

Juice of 1 lime

1 teaspoon sea salt

2 teaspoons finely chopped garlic

For the Ravioli

1 pound lump crabmeat, picked over for shells and broken up with a fork

1 tablespoon plus 1 teaspoon freshly grated peeled ginger

½ cup finely chopped cilantro

1 tablespoon freshly squeezed lime juice

Flour for dusting

20 egg roll wrappers (5¾-by-6¼-inches)

1 large egg and 1 teaspoon water, beaten together

MAKE THE DRESSING: Whisk all the ingredients for the dressing together in a measuring cup until the salt dissolves.

MAKE THE RAVIOLI: Combine the crabmeat, ginger, cilantro, and lime juice in a bowl and mix well.

Place an egg roll wrapper on a lightly floured work surface and place a rounded tablespoon of the crabmeat mixture in the center.

Using a pastry brush, paint a thick circle of egg wash all around the filling, fold the wrapper in half on the diagonal to create a triangle, and press down all along the

---

Hors d'Oeuvres: I always advise our dinner guests of the evening's menu and as the hors d'oeuvres are served, so too much nibbling won't interfere with appetites. And when I know the meal will be quite filling, I only plan a few tasty canapés— which is usually the case when I'm serving a beef dish. Selections of different of types of olives and fancy flavored ones are so readily available today that offering an interesting assortment in attractive bowls —with as many conveniently placed little dishes for the discarded pits—is ideal. Serve with a choice of nuts—from the humble peanut to the elegant macadamia and favorite almond—that come plain, salted, honey coated or spiced. And crunchy cheese sticks that are a current favorite in varied flavors and seasonings make a nice addition presented in tall glasses.

If you feel the occasion requires something made at home, try wrapping slices of proscuitto around pitted prunes that have been marinated overnight in some brandy— they'll be a wonderful contrast to the cheese sticks. For this menu, you should allow 18 pitted prunes that have soaked overnight in a half a cup of brandy. Cut nine slices of domestic proscuitto in half, and wrap each around a prune and secure with a toothpick.

edges to seal closed. Trim to a half-moon shape using a sharp knife or half of a 4½-inch fluted pastry cutter. Put the ravioli on a platter and continue until all 20 wrappers are used, placing a layer of cheesecloth or a light tea towel over each layer of ravioli as you work. (Leftover filling can be stored in an airtight container in the refrigerator for up to one day.) Refrigerate for at least 30 minutes and up to 2 hours. Bring back to room temperature before proceeding.

Bring a saucepan of salted water and a splash of oil to a boil, reduce the heat to maintain a low boil, and gently slide in the ravioli. Cook for 2 minutes, remove the pan from the heat, and drain the ravioli in colander.

Serve on plates and drizzle with the dressing.

Prime Rib Roast

$\mathcal{T}$he beef is cooked at a constant temperature of 325°F and with a Polder Thermo-Timer meat thermometer. Remove the roast from the oven when its internal temperature registers 125°F; it reaches the medium-rare temperature of 130°F as it rests before carving.

> Vegetable oil
> Kosher salt or coarse sea salt
> Freshly cracked black peppercorns
> Bunch of fresh thyme sprigs
> 4-rib roast (9 to 10 pounds), ribs cut from the meat,
>   replaced, and tied together with the meat
> Extra-virgin olive oil

Preheat the oven to 325°F, setting the rack at the lower-middle level. Grease a foil-lined roasting pan with vegetable oil.

Sprinkle salt and pepper on the bottom of the pan and scatter the thyme over.

Place the meat in the pan, bone side down, and rub all over with olive oil to coat thoroughly. Sprinkle salt and peppercorns over the sides and ends of the roast. Insert the Polder Thermo-Timer in the center of the roast, half way into the meat.

Place the pan in the oven, carefully arrange the lead wire from the thermometer, setting the temperature panel outside and close the oven door. Set the temperature on the thermometer for 130°F for medium-rare, or 125°F if you prefer to let the temperature reach 130°F while the roast is resting outside the oven (remember that the meat will continue to cook and its internal temperature will rise while it is resting).

Roast for 2¾ to 3 hours, basting with pan drippings once or twice, or until the meat's internal temperature registers 125° to 130°F. Remove from the oven, and transfer the roast to a carving board. Cover loosely with foil, set in a warm place away from drafts, and let the roast rest for 15 minutes before carving.

If you are making the Yorkshire Pudding (see opposite) drain the pan drippings into a heatproof measuring cup and set aside. Increase the oven temperature to 400°F and finish the pudding as described.

Yorkshire Pudding

Ironstone china was developed as a substitute for porcelain in early nineteenth century England. As it could be mass produced cheaply, it was a popular material for all types of pottery—from tableware to chamber pots.

A display of ironstone pieces contain an array of dried fruits, vegetables, and nuts that have been sprayed silver. The giant plastic 3 foot plus ornament and a few other over-sized ones (opposite) are an imitation of early mercury glass ornaments. As ironstone was an alternative to porcelain, mercury glass was considered a silver substitute and often called "a poor man's silver."

1 cup whole milk

1 cup all-purpose flour

1 teaspoon salt

2 large eggs

Reserved pan drippings from roast

Note: A pan for Yorkshire pudding has wells about 1 inch deep, you can substitute a muffin pan and fill the wells to three-quarters of an inch or use a muffin-top pan with shallower wells and fill as you would the Yorkshire pudding pan.

Combine the milk and 1 cup water in a measuring cup and mix.

Sift the flour and salt together into a large mixing bowl and make a well in the center. Drop in the eggs and mix. Gradually pour half of the milk mixture into the eggs, stirring in a widening circle out from the center, bringing the flour into the milk and water until well combined. Add the rest of the milk mixture and whisk until frothy and airy with bubbles.

Cover the bowl with a plate and set batter aside to rest at room temperature for at least 1 hour.

(Meanwhile, after the rib roast comes out of the oven, preheat the oven to 400°F.)

Pour 1 tablespoon of the roast's pan drippings into each well of a Yorkshire pudding pan or muffin pan and place in the hot oven until the drippings sizzle and are very hot. Remove the pan from the oven, quickly ladle batter on top of the hot drippings in each well until they are three-quarters full, and return the pan to the oven.

Bake until the puddings have risen above the tops of the wells, about 30 minutes. Remove from the oven and arrange on a serving platter.

Whipped Creamed Horseradish Sauce

❧

Horseradish sauce goes well with lots of things—roasted beef tenderloin, grilled steaks, venison, and smoked fish. Because I like to use it regularly, I have a few different recipes, one as simple and quick as a combination of 5 tablespoons prepared horseradish, ½ cup sour cream, a squeeze of lemon, and some salt and pepper, stirred together with a fork. This one is a bit more work, but well worth the effort.

You will have some sauce left over: it can be refrigerated in an airtight container for a few days.

Cups and saucers are popular items to collect. As there are special shapes and sizes for tea and different types of coffee drinks as well as myriad patterned designs to choose from, a collection can be varied. Some collections are quite specific and focus on the beverage, a theme for the pattern—such as floral or blue and white—others by the date of production or name of manufacture. In a very extensive collection, the former choices could be just a sub-category. Here, a collection is defined by its specific drink and by theme for their printed patterns. These demitasse cups are ornamented with traditional Christmas motifs—the decorated tree, branches of holly, holiday bells, and snowy landscape—that are equally as popular featured on greeting cards, gift wrap papers, and table linens as they are on all sorts of china and ceramics. Taking coffee after dessert in cups that match or mix holiday patterns is a festive note on which to end the Christmas dinner.

⅔ cup prepared horseradish (5 ounces), drained

2 tablespoons freshly squeezed lemon juice

½ teaspoon dry mustard powder

½ teaspoon sea salt

½ teaspoon freshly ground white pepper

2 cups heavy cream

Combine the horseradish, lemon juice, mustard, salt, and white pepper in a mixing bowl and set aside.

Put the cream in a deep bowl and whip with an electric hand mixer on medium speed until stiff peaks form.

Fold the horseradish mixture into the whipped cream and chill in the refrigerator for at least 30 minutes. Transfer to a serving bowl and pass alongside the rib roast at the table.

Creamed Baby Spinach and Watercress

Sea salt
2½ to 3 pounds baby leaf spinach, rinsed
½ pound watercress, trimmed of thick stems
4 tablespoons unsalted butter
6 tablespoons finely chopped shallots
2 tablespoons all-purpose flour
½ cup heavy cream, warmed slightly
⅛ to ¼ teaspoon ground nutmeg (optional)
Freshly ground black pepper

Bring a large saucepan of salted water to a boil and add the spinach and watercress. Bring the liquid back to a boil and cook for 1 to 2 minutes. Remove the pan from the heat and immediately drain the greens in a colander placed in the kitchen sink. Rinse quickly with cold water and drain well. Using the back of a wooden spoon, squeeze out as much liquid as possible.

Transfer the greens to the bowl of a food processor and pulse a few times, until they are just coarsely chopped.

Return the greens to the colander and squeeze out any remaining excess liquid. (The recipe can be prepared up to this point and finished later the same day if placed in an airtight plastic container—do not use metal—and stored in the refrigerator or a cool place. Bring the greens back to room temperature before continuing.)

Heat 1 tablespoon of the butter in a nonstick sauté pan or wok, add the shallots, and cook over medium heat until they are transparent, about 1 to 2 minutes. Add the chopped greens and cook, stirring, for 2 minutes, until heated through. Sprinkle the flour over the greens and mix well, working quickly. Cook until the spinach is hot, then remove the pan from the heat and blend in the warm cream.

Return the pan to the heat, bring to a simmer, and season with salt, pepper, and nutmeg if desired. Serve hot.

Chocolate Mousse
with Fresh Raspberries

———❦———

A chocoholic's version of comfort food must be a rich creamy mousse like this one. Serve each portion with a spoonful of refreshingly sweet-tart raspberries and a sprinkling of chopped mint leaves.

16 ounces sweetened dark chocolate, broken into small pieces

4 tablespoons unsalted butter

10 eggs, separated

2 tablespoons Armagnac or other fine brandy

1 quart fresh raspberries

Dark chocolate shavings (optional)

⅓ cup chopped mint (optional)

Confectioners' sugar (optional)

Combine the chocolate, butter, and 2 tablespoons plus 2 teaspoons water in a large heatproof bowl and set on top of a saucepan of simmering water—do not let the pan touch the water. Cook, stirring, until the mixture is smooth and creamy. Take the bowl off the pan and add the egg yolks one at a time, stirring constantly with a wooden spoon. Once the yolks have been thoroughly incorporated, stir in the Armagnac and set aside.

Using a wire whisk or electric hand mixer, beat the egg whites until stiff peaks form. Using a metal spoon, gently fold the egg whites into the chocolate mixture. Ladle the mixture into a serving bowl and refrigerate overnight or longer. (Cover with plastic wrap only if your refrigerator is full of things that could taint the taste of the mousse, otherwise leave uncovered, to prevent moisture from accumulating on the mousse.)

Decorate the mousse with chocolate shavings, some raspberries, and mint, and a sprinkling of confectioners' sugar if desired. Serve well chilled, spooning out the portions at the table with some raspberries on the side.

Christmas Breakfast: I don't think there's a morning that bustles with so much activity so early as that of Christmas, particularly if there are young children or the Peter Pan kind of adult around. Breakfast is best made up of finger food that's ready to serve on a help-yourself basis. Munching on biscuits stuffed with thin slices of prosciutto, berry-filled muffins that can be purchased or French toast quartered into squares that are quick to make and sprinkled with cinnamon and topped with a dollop of apple butter allows the squeals of joy and delight to ring around the tree without much interruption—and with little work for you. Hazelnut perfumed coffee for the grown-ups and hot chocolate with a peppermint stick for swizzling for the kids will wash down things nicely.

The Christmas breakfast table should be given as much attention for its festive decoration as the one for lunch or dinner on that day. Everyone will love to start the day surrounded by Frosty and all his snowmen friends. On the table, filling the shelves that line a bay window and outside the window, are snowmen figures old and new. While the characteristics of snowmen are fairly consistent—black top hat, eyes of coal, carrot or coal nose and optional scarf or broom—the materials they are made of are more diverse. Cotton batting and composite usually indicate the older snowmen. Pottery and wood have been widely used through the years, and plastic since it was first used to produce novelties.

Boxing Day Dinner

SERVES 6

HORS D'OEUVRES
Quail Eggs Two Ways

•

STARTER
*Lime and Peppercorn–Marinated Salmon
with Endive Salad*

CHAMPAGNE BOLLINGER

•

MAIN COURSE
Pheasant with Vin Jaune Sauce and Cipollini

•

SIDES
Polenta "Toasts"

French Green Beans

GEVREY-CHAMBERTIN

•

DESSERT
Baby Stilton Cheese and Crackers

Poached Pears

PORT

DURING THE YEARS WE LIVED IN LONDON WE ADDED England's holidays to our long list of American and French celebrations. One that particularly suited our efforts in prolonging the joys of Christmas was Boxing Day, a legal holiday that falls the day or first weekday after Christmas. The holiday formalized the giving of gifts or tips to those in service—and provided a day off for their own celebrations.

In our small circle of friends, it was considered an ideal time to get together for feasting and exchanging gifts, as December 25 was reserved for our family celebrations. The challenge, of course, was to come up with a menu that was as special as the preceding day's, but offered exciting alternatives to the traditional turkey, goose or roast beef that would most likely have been served. As a child, I remember being very impressed by the dish named "pheasant under glass" and wondering how it was eaten—it sounded challenging if not downright dangerous. Having tasted many great pheasant dishes over the years, I have come to appreciate this game bird for its natural elegance. Whenever it was my turn to host Boxing Day, I found pheasant the perfect choice for creating a special dinner.

MENU: *P*heasant is a special bird meant for special occasions; roasted or braised pheasant has been considered an elegant dish for centuries. The ancient Romans reassembled the cooked bird with its feathers for a grand presentation, while in medieval times they were fancifully decorated, their legs and beaks painted with gold. Equal to this reputation, this pheasant dish uses a special golden wine called Vin Jaune. It is a very expensive wine with a character and color not unlike sherry but is worth its weight in gold, as the rich sauce it produces is exceptional and perfect for an occasion like this.

The quickly pan-grilled breast ensures that the best bit of the bird is cooked to perfection, while the leg meat has enriched the sauce and is served like a garnish. Another game bird is used for one of the hors d'oeuvres and turns eggs into an elegant treat. Quail eggs are served two ways, hard-boiled and scrambled on bread rounds. The marinated salmon is the perfect light appetizer, followed as it is by the rich pheasant and a fruit and cheese course. Serving the traditional Stilton cheese and passing the port at the end of the meal is a fitting finish for this particularly English occasion.

TABLE AND DECORATIONS: *E*vergreen swags and wreaths and a collection of miniature artificial Christmas trees are a natural and festive setting for wild game bird designs. The table's figurine centerpiece, the place settings of hand-painted china and silverware, and the framed antique prints on the walls of the dining room feature pheasants, quail, grouse and wood pigeons.

The aroma of chestnuts roasting, gingerbread baking, and mulled wine simmering are reminders of comforting Christmas treats; the scents of the holidays are as familiar as the images we associate with the season. Pine, juniper berries, cinnamon, clove, ginger, orange, frankincense, and myrrh are some of the scents frequently captured in traditional holiday potpourri and pomander or spice balls. As beautiful to look at as they are to smell, bowls and baskets of potpourri and fragrant balls hung like ornaments or displayed on stands decorate our homes and scent our rooms during the holidays with the perfumes of Christmas.

TRADITIONS: *A*lthough Boxing Day is strictly a British affair, its origins can be found in much earlier times. The tradition of offering household or public servants a present or monetary token of appreciation for their services at this time of year is long-standing—holiday tips and bonuses for staff are commonly given today. The "box"

in Boxing Day has nothing to do with fisticuffs; it refers to the container that held the gifts or collected donations that was opened on December 26.

I'm sure many people assume artificial trees to be a modern invention and just as many take the view that a fake tree is a poor and sorry substitute for the real thing. When visions of flashy silver aluminum trees, snow-white synthetic ones and even brush bristly evergreens dance in our heads, we immediately think of the 1960s. But we're off by a century. Artificial trees first appeared as early as the 1860s in England.

For the most part, early artificial trees were made from the feathers of geese or turkeys, but sometimes swans' feathers or elegant ostrich plumes would be used. The feathers would be wrapped with wires to form branches that were arranged to re-create the form of an evergreen tree—and the result are aptly called "feather trees." Small in scale—from a few inches to a few feet tall—they were set up on tables, side boards, and even windowsills. Artificial trees were decorated with ornaments just like their real counterparts; while the tiniest of them were decorated with miniature ornaments and candles scaled down to their size. Even though new, improved materials were developed, feather trees were still being produced during the 1950s in America.

Santa Claus, as we know him today, is not the first or the only figure to bring the Christmas gifts, nor was he always a jolly round character dressed in a fur-trimmed red suit who arrived on the rooftop in a sleigh drawn by reindeer and descended the chimney on December 24. That Santa was visualized for us by a combination of the Clement Moore poem, Thomas Nast's illustration and, it's said, Coca-Cola ads—a time span of a century. But that would be a simplistic view, as there are almost as many traditions of this nature and kind of holiday character as there are Santas on the streets and in shops at Christmastime today. Many began as pagan winter rituals and evolved over the millennia: there's Father Christmas, Kriss Kringle, Bels or Pelze-Nichols, Knecht Ruppert, and good ol' Saint Nicholas, just to mention a few names that may ring some jingle bells for us. Saint Nicholas is usually considered the father of all santas, and may have truly existed around the fourth or fifth century A.D. The Bishop of Myra—a tall and kindly man who rode a noble white horse dressed in his bishop's robe and miter— rewarded the good, brought gifts to the poor, and protected children. For these deeds and miracles performed, he became the patron saint of children and his feast day was celebrated on December 6. His spirit was believed to travel the land on

*A*ntique frosted bottle brush miniature trees are arranged behind an antique Santa with his reindeer drawn sleigh. Eight as the number of reindeer in Santa's team is attributed to the famous Moore poem, and that they are all accounted for in this 1900 Santa and sleigh vignette makes this a valued antique.

the eve of his feast day to bring gifts for the nice and a switch for the naughty—in some parts of the world presents are still exchanged on this day. Some traditions had it that the saint was accompanied by a strange little creature who left the switch to punish the bad kiddies or just helped out with duties unsuitable for a bishop—the origin of Santa's elves.

COLLECTIBLES: *M*iniature artificial trees and even "toy"-sized ones that would have been part of Christmas villages are of interest to collectors. Some miniature antique artificial trees dating from the first quarter of the twentieth century can still be had—and replicas of these as well as other styles can be found new. The small feather types that came with ornaments and were displayed under a decorative, protective glass dome are extremely special, and it's difficult to acquire larger ones with their authentic decorations.

Santa is the most popular symbol of Christmas for collectors. His image appears on a wide variety of objects in equally as diverse materials: cards, tree ornaments, candy containers, toys, banks, jugs, mugs, cookie jars, and even cigarette lighters. While Santa items exist earlier, those produced from the 1870s to the early decades of the twentieth century offer an abundance of choice.

*H*unt country is the name for the style of this dining room, and wild birds the game that decorate the walls with antique prints and the table in the form of pheasant figurines and china patterned with game bird images—even the 1930s silverware is patterned with an engraved feather design. For Christmas, a forest woodland theme is carried out in the deep green table linens and holiday bows. A collection of tiny artificial trees that date as early as the 1900s and as late as today are used as the table's centerpiece and are scattered around the room amongst birch bark–wrapped candles. Scents of Christmas fill the air with displays of pomander balls made of clove-spiked oranges, and twig baskets filled with birch bark and potpourri.

At the start of the evenings festivities, a collection of tall glasses, decorated with a variety of Christmas tree designs and dating from the 1950s and 60s, were used for cocktails.

Quail Eggs Two Ways

Quail's eggs are available or can be ordered at some poulterers and many specialty food stores.

> 6 to 8 (6 ¼-inch) slices whole-grain or wheat bread
>
> 36 quails eggs, at room temperature
>
> 1 tablespoon crème fraîche or sour cream
>
> 2 tablespoons finely chopped cilantro
>
> 1 tablespoon unsalted butter
>
> ⅛ cup caviar or salmon roe (optional)
>
> 12 (¼-inch) rounds sliced scallions

Trim away the crusts from the bread slices and, using a 2-inch round pastry cutter, cut out 24 rounds. Set aside.

Bring a small saucepan of water to a boil and gently lower in 24 of the eggs with a large spoon, a few at a time. Turn off the heat, cover the pan, and let stand for 4 minutes. Remove the eggs from the pan and transfer them to a bowl of cold water. As soon as they are cool enough to handle, peel 16 of the eggs, reserving the rest for decoration of the platter.

Arrange the peeled boiled eggs, the unpeeled ones, and 12 bread rounds in an attractive pattern on a serving platter. Set aside.

Combine the remaining 12 quail eggs, the crème fraîche, and cilantro in a bowl and whisk with a fork. Melt the butter in a small nonstick sauté pan, over medium heat. Add the egg mixture to the pan and cook, pushing the eggs into soft mounds until the eggs are set but still moist. Transfer the scrambled eggs to a bowl, then spoon equal portions onto the remaining bread rounds and place on the platter. Top each portion with a small dollop of caviar if desired, and place a slice of scallion in the center of each. Serve immediately.

Against the backdrop of the artificial bottle-brush trees from the early twentieth century, are a pair of silver metal quail figurines from the beginning of the twenty-first century that complement the dish to be served—hard-boiled and scrambled quail's eggs. The pheasant design platter is mid-twentieth century.

Lime and Peppercorn–Marinated Salmon with Endive Salad

—✻—

This recipe requires the center cut of salmon, so that the fillet is at least three quarters of an inch thick at the thick end; and the fish must be very fresh. The salmon is not sliced in the traditional manner, which requires nearly expert skill, but in a much easier way: ⅛- to ⅜-inch slices are cut down the length of the fillets.

If you feel unsure about serving a fish prepared by yourself in this manner, purchase prepared gravlax or smoked salmon available from specialty food shops. Serve with rounds of endive dressed with some purchased mustard dill sauce for the gravlax and a sour cream and fresh chive topping (8 ounces of sour cream to 1 tablespoon of chopped chives) for the smoked fish.

For the Salmon
2 tablespoons plus 1 teaspoon extra-virgin olive oil
⅔ cup freshly squeezed lime juice
¼ cup finely chopped chives
1 tablespoon black peppercorns, coarsely cracked
1 tablespoon green peppercorns, coarsely cracked
1 teaspoon sea salt
2 pounds fresh center-cut salmon fillets (¾-inch-thick, skinned)

For the Endive Salad
½ cup extra-virgin olive oil
¼ cup freshly squeezed lime juice
1 tablespoon finely chopped chives
Sea salt
Freshly ground black pepper
4 heads endive, trimmed and sliced into ¼-inch rounds
12 stems fresh chives, cut in half

Answering the question "Where does Santa come from?" with "the North Pole" is as simplistic as replying "from the cabbage patch!" to that of "Where do babies come from?" While Saint Nicholas, the Bishop of Myra, is the quasi-historical figure considered to be the forerunner of all later "Santas," connections can be made between pagan figures in ancient rituals and the saint and his successors.

When Protestant churches suppressed devotion to saints, the gift-bearing figure became the Christ Child, or a more secular and often harsh personality, and unlike the saint they visited on December 24. Father Christmas was the image of a kind man dressed in a monklike robe—he was not a religious character, but a personification of the Christmas feast. Pelznickel (fur-Nicholas) Knecht Ruppert and Ru-Klas (rough-Nicholas) were stern and even ugly, frightening figures that admonished and punished the naughty. They blended some of the Nicholas character with that of the sprites, elves, and devilish companions of the ancient gods of the yule and Saturnalia feasts.

The Santas (and some Father Christmases) on these shelves come from every country that has had a Christmas industry, in almost every form that Santa's image has been used. Created over a period of 110 years—the oldest dates from 1890—they're cards, scrap, books, calendars, lamps, stockings, door knob covers, rugs, candlesticks, toys, and, of course, candy containers and tree ornaments. They make music, they move, they pop up like a jack-in-the-box—and come with their signature sleigh, reindeer, sack or a chimney.

(continued)

Make the Salmon: Combine the oil, lime juice, chives, peppercorns, and salt in a bowl and mix together. Arrange the salmon in a shallow nonreactive baking dish, pour the marinade over, and turn over a few times so the fish is evenly coated. Cover with plastic wrap and refrigerate for 5 hours. Remove the salmon from the refrigerator and place on a cutting board; discard the marinade. Cut the salmon down its length into ⅛- to ⅜-inch slices and divide among individual serving plates, placing the slices down the center of the plate.

Make the Endive Salad: Combine the oil, lime juice, chives, and salt and pepper in a measuring cup and mix well. Put the endive rounds around the edges of the serving plates, around the sliced salmon. Whisk the dressing and drizzle it over the endives. Garnish with the stems of chives and serve.

Pheasant with Vin Jaune Sauce and Cipollini

The cooking of the pheasant can be challenging indeed, if the meat is not properly handled. As with all poultry cooked whole, the fact that the breast or white meat finishes cooking before the dark meat poses a potential problem—one will be too dry by the time the other is finally cooked. Added to that, as with most wild game, the pheasant's diet and lifestyle result in more muscle and less of the fatty tissue that keeps the meat moist during cooking and adds considerable flavor. The easy solutions are to cook the breast and legs separately, by two different methods, and to use farm-raised but free-range pheasant hens (cocks take longer to cook). In this recipe the breasts are pan-fried and the legs are braised in a special wine—Vin Jaune—to create a rich sauce. The breasts and legs marinate together; a stock can be made from the rest.

Farm-raised free-range pheasants are readily available from late September to mid-April (see page 162 for sources). Vin Jaune is a special and very expensive wine with a character and color not unlike sherry available or to order at quality

This detail of the main picture on the previous page features santas bearing Christmas presents—arriving at their destination on the night of December 24 with at sack full of gifts even on skis. The tradition is said to find its roots in one of the stories about the life of the original St. Nicholas—the Bishop of Myra.

Legend has it that the three daughters of a recently empoverished man hadn't enough money for their dowries and so wouldn't be able to marry, living out their lives as poor spinsters— or worse. One night the saint passed by the open window of their house and tossed in a bag of gold coins. With this kind act, the eldest daughter was able to marry. Nicholas repeated his nocturnal visit twice more, each time, "delivering" a bag of gold for the remaining sisters. This charming story of St. Nick's generous gifts established him as the bringer of presents on his feast day as well as making him the patron saint of pawnbrokers—the symbol of three gold balls that mark their shops referring to the three bags of gold in the story.

wine shops. It produces an exceptional sauce for a special occasion like this. If you find it's too dear, use a fine red Burgundy instead.

three (3-pound) free-range pheasant hens, quartered (your butcher or poulterer will do this for you, ask him to bone the breasts and trim the end bones of legs)

For the Marinade

1 large onion, chopped

2 large shallots, chopped

2 large cloves garlic, crushed

3 carrots, scraped and chopped

1 bouquet garni (4 sprigs parsley, 2 or 3 sprigs thyme, and 1 bay leaf tied together)

1 bottle Vin Jaune (or fine red Burgundy) or 750 ml. of light dry sherry

For the Cipollini

3 tablespoons unsalted butter

½ pound pancetta or smoked bacon, cut into 1-by-¼-inch strips

18 to 24 cipollini, peeled, trimmed, and scored at the bottom (or 1-inch white boiling onions)

For the Pheasant

Sea salt

Freshly ground black pepper

3 to 4 tablespoons vegetable oil

4 tablespoons flour

⅓ cup cognac

6 to 8 tablespoons unsalted butter

MAKE THE MARINADE: In a large bowl or nonreactive baking dish, combine the onion, shallots, garlic, carrots, and the bouquet garni. Pour in the wine and stir. Add the pheasant pieces and turn to coat thoroughly. Arrange the legs at the bottom and the breasts on top. Cover with plastic wrap and let marinate at room temperature for 4 hours (6 hours if refrigerated). Remove the pheasant pieces from the marinade, transferring the breasts and legs onto separate plates, and reserve the marinade. Cover the meat, minus the legs, which stay out for cooking, with plastic wrap and refrigerate.

(continued)

MAKE THE CIPOLLINI: Preheat the oven to 200°F, setting the first rack at the lowest level and the second rack at the middle.

Melt 1 tablespoon of the butter in a large sauté pan and cook the pancetta until crisp and golden brown. With a slotted spoon, remove the pancetta from the pan, drain on paper towels, and set aside.

Add the cipollini to the pan and cook over medium-high heat until lightly browned. Pour in enough water to come halfway up their sides, add the remaining 2 tablespoons butter, cover, and simmer for 25 minutes. At that time the cipollini should be tender; uncover, increase the heat, and boil off any remaining liquid. Remove from the heat, transfer to an ovenproof dish, and cover with foil. Set aside in the warm oven until ready to use.

COOK THE PHEASANT: Wipe away any bits of marinade vegetables from the pheasant legs, pat dry, and season with salt and pepper.

Heat the oil in a flameproof casserole or Dutch oven. Working in batches if necessary, add the legs a few at a time and cook until golden on all sides; remove the pieces to a platter and set aside.

Add 2 tablespoons of the flour to the casserole and cook for 2 to 3 minutes, stirring constantly; remove from the heat.

Meanwhile, warm the cognac in a separate saucepan or in a microwave oven.

Return the pheasant legs to the casserole, add the cognac, and light it with a match. When the flames have subsided, put the casserole back on the heat and add the marinade. Bring the liquid to a boil over high heat. Reduce the heat to maintain a simmer and cook, partially covered, for 35 minutes.

Meanwhile, wipe away any bits of the marinade vegetables from the pheasant breasts and pat dry. Heat a large heavy skillet over medium-high heat, add some of the butter, and let the pan get hot. Add a few of the breasts, skin side down, and cook for 4 minutes on each side. Don't overcrowd the pan. Wrap each breast in some foil as they finish cooking and keep warm in the oven with the cipollini.

Test the pheasant legs for doneness, piercing deep into the thigh with a fork; the juices should run pale pink. Continue cooking for 10 to 15 minutes longer, until the juices run clear after testing. Remove the pheasant from the casserole, remove the skin and discard, cut the meat off the bone and shred onto a plate. Cover with foil, and keep warm in the oven with the breasts and the cipollini.

Pour the cooking liquid through a sieve into a large measuring cup and discard the solid bits. Pour the liquid back into the casserole and bring to a boil.

In a small bowl, combine the flour with 2 tablespoons of the butter and work the mixture into a *beurre manié* with a fork or your fingers.

While Santa is very often depicted caught in the act of climbing down the chimney or driving his sleigh loaded down with a sack full of toys, variations on those themes do exist. Santa slips into his own big boot in a pottery piece from the late 1940s—his boots have been immortalized, too, as candy containers and planters. And he delivers the family tree by early aeroplane—probably a 1930s creation. Modern times were reflected in Santa figures—he's been seen traveling by train, car, and even hot air balloon.

The tradition of putting out some cookies and milk for Santa and carrots for his reindeer when they visit on Christmas Eve is a long-standing one

Remove the casserole from the heat. Whisk some of the hot sauce into the bowl with the flour and butter mixture. When it is smooth, whisk the mixture into the sauce in the casserole and blend until smooth and thoroughly incorporated.

Return the casserole to the heat, add the pancetta, cipollini, and sliced dark meat, and bring to a simmer to heat through.

Serve the breast hot with the cipollini, some leg meat, and the Polenta Toasts and Haricort Verts (see page 157) with some sauce spooned over.

Polenta "Toasts"

of great charm (see page 159 for a cookie recipe for Santa). Finding crumbs and an empty glass the next morning was proof positive he was real. I was thrilled by this custom as a child, and I have been thrilled watching the children's reaction as an adult. So what better motif for a cookie jar than Santa's jovial face. Father Christmas in his long robe is the model for these salt-and-pepper shakers. By the way, the less popular character of Mrs. Claus didn't appear until 1889, when Katherine Lee Bates created her for "Goody Santa Claus on a Sleigh Ride"—Ms. Bates was also the author of "America the Beautiful"!

Alan Rodford introduced me to pheasant served with bread fried in butter and some herbs—a dish he loved to make at his Cambridgeshire week-end cottage. I use polenta slices as a flavorful substitute.

1 recipe Polenta Loaf at room temperature (see page 157)
3 to 4 tablespoons unsalted butter, plus additional if needed
Freshly ground black pepper
2 tablespoons chopped thyme

Cut the polenta into 24 ¼-inch slices. Melt the butter in a large nonstick skillet over medium-high heat. As the butter foams, sprinkle it with some salt and pepper and a pinch of the thyme, then add some of the polenta slices and season the top with salt, pepper, and thyme. Fry the slices until golden on each side.

Baby Stilton Cheese and Poached Pears

I was introduced to the great British tradition of Stilton—which would be served after the dessert course in a formal meal—by our friend J. R. Bullen during our years in London. With a glass of fine port, it's a wonderful complement to a cooked-fruit course served before or after the cheese and crackers.

For the Pears

> 3 cups red wine
>
> 1½ cups sugar
>
> 1 cup honey
>
> ¼ cup freshly squeezed lemon juice
>
> 2 (1-inch) cinnamon sticks
>
> 6 just-ripe red Clapp pears, washed and cored

The Cheese

> 1 whole baby or midget Stilton cheese
>
> Water biscuits, whole-meal crackers, and soda crackers

Combine the wine, sugar, honey, lemon juice, and cinnamon sticks in a large saucepan. Bring to a simmer and add the pears. Cover tightly and gently simmer for 10 to 15 minutes, until the pears are quite tender, offering no resistance when pierced with the tip of a knife.

Remove the pears from the pan, arrange upright on a serving plate, and let cool.

Cut the top ¼ inch of the cylinder of Stilton off in one piece, reserving the top for use as a cover for the cheese. Using a spoon, scoop out portions of cheese, working from the center to the sides; or cut wedges of cheese by cutting horizontally ¼ inch down and then slicing small pielike servings from the center.

Pass the crackers and port around the table.

The countdown to Christmas Day can seem an eternity to children, but not if the Advent days are spent in creating their own decorations—as was often the case for both young and old in the past. This antique feather tree is decorated with some handmade if not homemade ornaments, assembled from kits or created with personal artistry. The geometric shaped and patterned boxes date from the late 1800s and are put together each year for the tree—as are the paper cones and bird house. The little book named for Martha is made of whale-bone and holds pins. From the 1920s and 30s are a dragonfly made of celluloid and wire, a cotton doll, and some glass ornaments—a Dresden star (ca. 1900) tops the tree. Below, a modern Santa rug, hand hooked the old fashioned way.

Twelfth Night in Town

SERVES 6

HORS D'OEUVRES
Crudités with Dip
Mom's Miniature Potato Pancakes

•

STARTER
Cream of Watercress Soup

SAINT-VÉRAN

•

MAIN COURSE
Medley of Mushroom and Asparagus Tip Vol-au-Vents

•

SIDE
Wilted Swiss Chard

SAUMUR ROUGE

•

DESSERT
Gâteaux des Roi

CHAMPAGNE RUINART

On the twelfth day of Christmas
my true love gave to me . . .

———————✿———————

Although Christmas Day may come but once a year, there are twelve days to this holiday's period of festivities—and more if you start your celebrations early. You can launch the season by celebrating the old feast day of Saint Nicholas or start with Sweden's tradition of Saint Lucia's Day, which falls a week later. Otherwise, kick off with the traditional Christmas Eve.

My Christmas calendar has yet to include the two early feasts, but it does extend to January 5, when my family celebrates the Epiphany. That date commemorates the arrival in Bethlehem of the three kings from the East and their presentation of gifts to honor the infant Jesus. While the Twelfth Night brings those Three Kings, the day after brings twelve drummers drumming, according to the carol—and an official end to the season as custom has it. My husband's family is of French origin, so we celebrate Epiphany and the arrival of the kings with a special Twelfth Night dinner. It's a way to celebrate the many days of Christmas and bring the season to a close.

Menu: Vegetarianism is a growing trend, and many of us now enjoy meatless meals a few times a week both for taste preferences and dietary or health concerns. The dishes here, although not suitable for vegans, are appropriate for most vegetarians and will be enjoyed by those taking a break from the overabundance of roasted meats and poultry usually offered at holiday tables. Offer a plate of cauliflower florets, grape tomatoes, and baby carrots with any good-quality purchased dip and some miniature potato pancakes as hors d'oeuvres and follow with the watercress soup. Serving the Vol-au-Vent as individual pastry shells surrounded by the vegetable greens makes a wonderful presentation appropriate to a special dinner. The French Twelfth Night Cake is usually presented as a single large cake, but is made as small individual ones here. As just one of the cakes will contain the favor— offer them on a platter and allow your guests to choose their own little gâteau, making the serving of dessert part of the ritual.

TABLE AND DECORATIONS: *I*deas for decorating the home and the table at Christmas so often concentrate on creating an old-fashioned country charm or an antique romanticism, excluding or at least marginalizing those more urban or modern in look. While I relish decorating our country home in a rather traditional manner, I truly enjoy the alternative style our city loft allows me to explore.

That style focuses on the urban setting of the studio's location and its cityscape views, an interior décor dominated by my husband's profession and passion—photography—and our fondness for collecting things old-fashioned, modern, or whimsical.

The traditional holiday elements of red, evergreens, tree, ornaments, and a centerpiece for the holiday table are all present and feature New York City and the Empire State Building as a decorative theme. The streamlined 1930s color scheme of black and white with silver enhances Michel's collection of antique cameras and his framed photographs of New York City architecture and portraits of celebrities from Nashville—his other favorite town.

TRADITIONS: *A*s with so many other feast days, one can trace the date for the festival of the Epiphany back in time to pagan or other ancient religious rituals. Until the latter part of the fourth century, the Eastern Christian Church commemorated the birth and baptism of Jesus, as well as the first miracle at Cana on this date. The Epiphany celebration echoes earlier ancient festivals in Egypt, where the overflow of the Nile was celebrated, and other areas in the Middle East, where the miracle of water fountains flowing with wine were honored at this time.

When Constantinople eventually recognized December 25 as the date of Christ's birth, Epiphany became the celebration of His baptism accompanied by the blessing of waters and baptisms. The Church of Rome observed the date as the arrival of The Three Kings and the celebration of Christmas lasted twelve days.

While the twelfth day after Christmas marks the official end of the holiday season, it is the eve that was most often celebrated as a joyful night of festivity and merriment—a custom that continues today in many societies where the rituals of the evening's feasting and games were combined in a cake. The French version consists of a flaky pastry case with almond-paste filling, while the American one is the dense, heavily iced fruitcake typically associated with Christmas. In all cakes for Twelfth Night, the charm or favor—often a raw dried bean representing the Christ Child—is enclosed in the cake. The person who finds it is crowned "king" or "queen," with the right to choose a noble partner and lead in the evening's games.

The holiday holly and ivy that make their appearance as floral arrangements, garlands, and wreaths today trace their symbolic significance to ancient rituals, as do all the evergreens used for decoration at Christmas. Holly and ivy were believed to have magical powers and were seen as symbols of eternal life because they remained green throughout the changing seasons. Once banned by the Christian church, holly was later reinstated as "Christ's Thorn" and proclaimed to be the shrub from which Christ's crown of thorns was made—making this green sacred and suitable for Christmas. Ivy was encouraged to grow all over countryside cottages, as it was seen as a protection against evil spirits.

The symbolism of both greens is referred to in the old traditional carol "The Holly and the Ivy."

Everyone who celebrates Christmas has a space set aside in their attic, basement, or storage area filled with boxes of holiday decorations. And often the most beloved or precious objects in them will be the ornaments for the tree. Acquired over the years, ornaments mark the passage of time and commemorate special events in our lives.

The ornaments that decorated early Christmas trees were homemade from fruits, nuts, cookies, and candies. Colorful ribbons, candles, as well as paper chains and roses also could be found on early trees. And before the advent of gift-wrapping paper in the twentieth century, the family's presents were sometimes hung on the tree, often in cone-shaped containers called cosques or eggshells that were halved, gilded, and then filled. Homemade ornaments in the Victorian period were fashioned from printed cards, scrap or plain cardboard, and trimmed with tinsel, angel hair, lace, and gold paper to fanciful effect.

During the growth in popularity of the holiday tree over the centuries, the subjects used for the design of decorations and the materials from which they were made evolved and expanded greatly. Christmas figures, toys, musical instruments, bells, and beads were fashioned from wood, porcelain, papier-mâché, metals, cotton batting, and glass. And many of these factory produced baubles that re-created the early edible ornaments.

The Christmas-decorations industry was firmly established by the 1840s, and dominated by German manufacturers because of their preeminence in the production of toys. An order from 1848 for six dozen Christmas balls in three different sizes is the first record of glass ornaments being manufactured and sold, but by the 1890s these now ubiquitous decorations were widely distributed. In the late 1930s, the Shiny Brite company opened in the United States, and eventually became the largest producer of ornaments in the States, overtaking the German manufacturers' market position.

COLLECTIBLES: *O*ver time, ornaments have been subject to fads and fashions—so collectors of tree ornaments have a wide array of forms, design motifs, and materials from which to choose. Dresdens, made of gilded and embossed card molded in a variety of shapes and designs, can be singled out as the most exquisite of antique decorations with their intricate detailing but overall simplicity. Dresdens are rare and can be extremely valuable as they were produced for a short period of time—from around 1880 to 1910.

Many modern tree ornaments can rival the beauty and artistry of the old, and are equally as collectible as antique items. New ornaments are especially popular when they are elaborately decorated and intricately shaped or colored.

Those that are in the form of fun, familiar, or fantasy objects are charming and delightful and often collected by their subject or theme.

A black-and-white theme for the table brings together a collection of antique transferware, modern hand-painted side plates, and plain white china chargers. Christmas red and green provide festive accents—as do the holly and the ivy. The dinner plates and teacups with saucers are a mixture of similar—but not matching—transferware patterns produced by different Staffordshire companies and collected over the years. While the teacups are used for wine on this occasion, Christmas-red tumblers from the 1950s serve for the water. The silver buildings and snow globes—miniatures of New York City's architectural monuments and skyline that reflect the loft's cityscape views—are set in other transferware pieces filled with moss and Christmas ivy that trails out onto the table. Holiday holly leaves sit on black Wedgwood Jasperware ashtrays as a decorative detail, no longer needed for their original purpose. The holly motif appears on the bread plates and as place cards, cut out like old-fashioned silhouettes in black craft paper and attached to the napkins with silky black cord.

Mom's Miniature Potato Pancakes

My mother's celebrated recipe for potato pancakes is measured out to produce miniatures, perfectly scaled for canapés. Serve with bite-size raw vegetables—such as cauliflower florets, tiny tomatoes, and baby carrots—and a favorite good-quality vegetable or cheese dip like hummus or creamy blue cheese, purchased in advance.

> 2 pounds (3 to 4) large baking potatoes, peeled and grated
> 1 large onion, peeled and grated
> 1 egg, lightly beaten
> ¼ cup all-purpose flour
> Juice of 1 lemon
> ¾ teaspoon sea salt
> Freshly ground black pepper
> ¼ cup vegetable oil

Combine the potatoes, onion, egg, flour, lemon juice, and salt and pepper in a large bowl and mix well. Place a skillet or sauté pan over medium heat and pour in enough oil to make a film over the bottom of the pan. When the oil is hot and shimmering, mound 2 tablespoons of the potato mixture onto a spoon and then place it in the oil. Repeat until skillet is full—don't overcrowd the pan. Immediately press down on the mounds with a spatula to level into flat pancakes. Cook for 5 to 8 minutes on each side, until golden brown and crispy. Repeat until all the mixture is used, setting the pancakes aside on paper towels to drain.

If not serving immediately, arrange the pancakes on a baking sheet, and rewarm in 425°F oven. Serve hot.

Cream of Watercress Soup

3 tablespoons unsalted butter

2 large leeks, trimmed, washed, cut into ¼-inch rounds,
    washed again, and drained

1 medium sweet onion, thinly sliced

1 pound Yukon gold potatoes, peeled and thinly sliced

3 cups clear vegetable bouillon

1 cup whole milk

14-ounces watercress (2 bunches), washed, drained,
    tough and thick stems removed and coarsely chopped

½ teaspoon sea salt

Freshly ground black pepper

¼ cup heavy cream

2 egg yolks, lightly beaten

Melt the butter in a large heavy saucepan over medium heat, add
the leeks and onion, and cook, stirring frequently, until translucent,
about 5 minutes.

Add the potatoes and stir to coat them with butter; cook for 3 to
4 minutes. Pour in the vegetable bouillon, adding some water if the
liquid does not cover the potatoes. Partially cover, and cook for 20 to
25 minutes, until the potatoes are very tender and cooked through.

Add 3 cups water, the milk, watercress, salt and pepper, and
simmer, uncovered, for 15 minutes, stirring occasionally. Remove
from the heat and pass the mixture through a food mill or medium-
mesh sieve into a large bowl, pressing down with the back of a
wooden spoon. Pour the puree back into the pan and place over
medium heat to warm through.

Meanwhile, in a small bowl, blend the cream and the egg yolks
together with a whisk. When the soup has rewarmed, slowly pour
the cream mixture into the soup, whisking constantly. Heat the soup
over low heat, stirring, for 3 to 4 minutes, until hot. Do not let the
soup boil or it will get lumpy. Serve immediately.

Medley of Mushroom and Asparagus Tip Vol-au-Vents

You can purchase sheets of puff pastry dough, found in the freezer section of most supermarkets.

For the Pastry Cups

2 pounds fresh or frozen Puff Pastry Dough (page 158) defrosted overnight in the refrigerator if frozen

Unsalted butter

Flour for dusting

1 egg yolk plus 1 teaspoon water, beaten together

For the Filling

1 ounce dried morels, reconstituted in 2 cups warm water for 3 hours

2 tablespoons all-purpose flour

5 tablespoons unsalted butter

½ cup Marsala

2 cups heavy cream

3 tablespoons finely chopped shallots

½ to ¾ pound shiitake mushrooms, stems removed and discarded, caps cleaned and diced

½ to ¾ pound cremini (or white button) mushrooms, stems removed and discarded, caps cleaned and diced

½ cup chopped cooked asparagus (see page 156)

2 tablespoons finely chopped parsley

Freshly squeezed lemon juice

Sea salt

Freshly ground black pepper

MAKE THE PASTRY CUPS: Grease and lightly flour a baking sheet. Lightly flour a rolling pin and work surface. Cut the dough in half. Roll out half the dough to a rectangle of

(continued)

¼-inch thickness. Using a 4¾-inch fluted pastry cutter, cut out 12 circles of dough, then use a 2½-inch fluted cutter to cut out and remove a center circle from 6 of the dough circles. Transfer 6 bases (the 6 solid dough circles) to the prepared baking sheet.

Brush the edges of the dough bases with the egg wash; do the same for the 6 dough rings. Place the rings, wet side down, on top of the solid bases and press them together.

Gently pressing down with your finger, use the dull edge of a knife to make evenly spaced indentations all around the edges of the dough rings.

With a fork, make several pricks in the centers of the bases. Use a toothpick to pierce the pastry dough a few times at the center of the bottom and make 4 evenly spaced punctures on the top rings of the dough through to the baking sheet.

Place the 2½-inch pastry cutter inside the top ring of dough and gently press down on the cutter, making a ¹⁄₁₆-inch-deep circular incision into the base.

Put the baking sheet in the refrigerator and chill for 30 minutes. Remove from the refrigerator and brush the egg wash all over the dough circles.

Heat the oven to 400°F, setting the rack at the middle level.

Place the baking sheet in the oven and bake for 30 to 35 minutes, until the pastry cups have risen and are golden brown. Remove from the oven, let cool, and set aside. (The pastry cups can be made a few hours ahead, kept in a cool dry place.)

Make the Filling: Although it is best to prepare the filling toward the end of the pastry-cup baking time so it can be spooned into the cups while warm, it can be prepared ahead, brought to room temperature, heated through in a pan, then put in the pastry cups.

Remove the rehydrated morels from their soaking liquid with a slotted spoon, pressing down on them with another spoon over the bowl. Place the mushrooms on a cutting board and set the soaking liquid aside. Coarsely chop the mushrooms.

In a small bowl, combine the flour with 2 tablespoons of the butter and work the mixture into a *beurre manié* with a fork or your fingers; set aside.

Heat 1 tablespoon of the butter in a sauté pan over low heat and add the morels. Increase the heat and cook for 2 minutes, stirring.

Pour in the Marsala, bring to a boil, and cook until the liquid is reduced by two-thirds. Add the 2 cups morel soaking liquid and boil for 5 minutes. Reduce the heat to a gentle simmer and pour in the cream. Cook for 15 minutes or until the sauce thickens, making sure that it does not boil. To achieve a rich, creamy consistency you may need to add some or all of the *beurre manié*. Whisk one-third of the *beurre manié* into the sauce over low heat, then simmer, stirring, for 3 minutes. Add another third and repeat as necessary to thicken the sauce.

Bringing home fresh cut evergreen branches of holly is the image of the 1930s printed crepe paper (opposite top). Holly and its berries trace their symbolic significance for Christmas to ancient rituals, as do all the evergreens used for decoration at Christmas. Viewed as a symbol of eternal life because it remained ever green throughout the changing seasons, holly was believed to have magical powers and was considered sacred having been the shrub from which Christ's crown of thorns was made. Many holiday objects feature holly's branches, leaves, and berries either combined with other holiday greens and the Christmas robin, or on their own, as seen in this late Victorian glass pitcher and tumbler set.

Meanwhile, heat the remaining 2 tablespoons butter in a large sauté pan over low heat and add the shallots. Cook for 1 to 2 minutes, until translucent; do not let them brown. Add the shiitake and cremini mushrooms, increase the heat to medium, and cook for 8 minutes, stirring constantly. The mushrooms are done when they are tender. Stir in the asparagus and parsley and continue cooking for 3 minutes. Reduce the heat to low and season to taste with lemon juice, salt, and pepper.

Pour in the sauce and cook for 2 minutes. Turn off the heat. Have the bottoms of the baked pastry cups—at room temperature or just warm—set out on individual serving plates. Spoon equal portions of the mushroom filling into the pastry cups, top with the pastry lids, and arrange the Wilted Swiss Chard (see below) around the Vol-au-Vents. Serve immediately.

Wilted Swiss Chard

3½ to 4 pounds rainbow Swiss chard, rinsed and drained
4 tablespoons extra-virgin olive oil
Sea salt
Freshly ground black pepper

Cut the Swiss chard leaves lengthwise on either side of the stems, and discard the stems. Pile up several leaves of similar size and roll them up from the ends. Holding the rolled-up leaves firmly, cut across the roll, making ¼-inch slices. Put the sliced chard in a large mixing bowl and repeat until all the leaves have been sliced.

Drizzle the oil over the chard and toss to coat evenly.

Heat a large nonstick sauté pan or wok over medium-high heat. Add half of the chard and cook, stirring. As the chard wilts, and there is more room in the pan, add the rest of the greens and cook, stirring, for 2 minutes.

Cover the pan and cook 3 minutes longer. Uncover, season with salt and pepper, and cook until most of the liquid has evaporated, 2 to 3 minutes more. Serve hot around the Vol-au-Vents.

Gâteaux des Roi

❦

$\mathcal{I}$n French tradition, the *Gâteau de Roi,* an almond paste–filled cake presented on Twelfth Night, has a charm or bean (representing the Christ Child) hidden in it. Whoever finds it in his slice of cake is declared king for the night. He or she may choose a queen or king and make a wish, which, of course, will be granted.

For the Filling

⅓ cup plus 1 tablespoon ground blanched almonds

⅓ cup plus 1 tablespoon sugar

2 egg yolks

1½ tablespoons unsalted butter, cut into small bits

4 tablespoons white rum

1 dried red kidney bean (for the charm)

For the Pastry

Flour for dusting

1 pound 6 ounces fresh or frozen Puff Pastry Dough (page 158) defrosted overnight in the refrigerator if frozen

Unsalted butter

1 egg plus 1 teaspoon water, beaten together

MAKE THE FILLING: Combine the almonds and sugar in a bowl, add the egg yolks, and mix together thoroughly. Add the butter and pound it into the mixture until well incorporated. Pour in the rum and continue to blend until the mixture is a coarse paste.

MAKE THE PASTRY: Preheat the oven to 400°F, setting the rack at the middle level.

Lightly flour a rolling pin and work surface. Roll out the pastry dough to a ⅜-inch thickness. Using a 4½-inch round pastry cutter, cut out 12 circles from the dough.

On a greased and lightly floured baking sheet, place 6 of the dough circles; drop 1 rounded teaspoon of the filling into the center of each. Place the dried bean in the paste of one of the cakes. Using a pastry brush, paint the egg wash all around

All tree ornaments do not have to be suspended from the branches of the Christmas tree. Nor do all decorated holiday trees have to be an evergreen or even a tree. A home can be dressed up for the Christmas season using a different approach — and to great festive effect.

A collection of beautiful and large modern day ornaments look equally as splendid suspended with colorful cords or ribbons from our loft ceiling's track lighting system as they would from a tree. Dangling above the dining table, they're as beautiful as any chandelier. If you're spending Christmas in the country or away from home—or if the aspect of bringing the tree in and out of your apartment is just something you'd rather not face—you may want to consider alternatives to a fresh cut tree. Cuttings of holiday greens or even branches stripped bare of their leaves are great to decorate. In the early tradition of homemade ornaments made from printed cards, I have fashioned picture postcards and playing cards that feature photographs of the Big Apple's skyscrapers into tiny decorations and hung them on branches gathered from the woods around our home in upstate New York. Miniature replicas of the buildings and the Statue of Liberty collected during our many visits with friends from abroad carry out a very New York state of design.

the filling. Place the remaining 6 dough circles on top of the bases and press down firmly all around the edge to seal.

Center a 3½-inch pastry cutter over one of the rounds and gently press down onto the dough but do not cut through. Using a small knife, working around the circumference of the dough circle, cut in from the edge to the cutter every ½-inch. Repeat the process with all 6 circles. Refrigerate the rounds for 30 minutes.

Remove from the refrigerator and paint the tops of each cake with the egg wash.

Using a sharp knife, make a ⅛-inch slit in the top of the cake at the center. Then draw curved lines, ⅛-inch deep, from the center to the edge, if you wish, to create a decorative design on top.

Brush the rounds again with the egg wash, being careful not to glaze over the center slit.

Immediately place in the oven and bake for 20 to 30 minutes, until the pastry has risen and the cakes are golden brown. They will slide easily off the baking sheet. Remove from the oven, let cool for 5 minutes, and serve.

Holiday Lunch

SERVES 4

HORS D'OEUVRES
Cheese Platter
Celery Sticks, Olives, and Nuts

•

STARTER
Pan-Grilled Duck Breasts on Field Greens
with Apple Cider Vinaigrette

•

MAIN COURSE
Braised Duck Legs
with Red Cabbage and Apples

•

SIDES
Sautéed Potatoes

CÔTE RÔTIE

•

DESSERT
Tarte Tatin

BANYULS

God rest ye merry gentlemen
Let nothing ye dismay . . .

———— 🧺 ————

THE HOLIDAY SEASON IS A TIME FOR GETTING TOGETHER with friends and neighbors, as well as family. In the month of December, our social calendars are filled in with school and church functions, informal open-house gatherings, parties, dinners, brunches, and lunches. Advice for entertaining on these occasions all too often overlooks the small and intimate celebrations that are also enjoyed during Christmas.

Over the years, sharing a quiet Sunday lunch midway through the season with our two closest friends became a welcome tradition. A jeans and "jumpers" (as the British call sweaters) casual affair, the afternoon was designed to be a relaxing break from the round of social commitments and Christmas preparations.

We devised a plan to guarantee that the day is as laid-back and lazy as it can be: we alternate hosting the lunch each year, and the guests provide the hors d'oeuvres and dessert, while the role of chef was assumed in rotation and he or she is guaranteed three sous chefs if needed. This division of labor always produces a quality meal and, as the expression goes, quality time together.

MENU: The dishes here are a snap with everyone pitching in, but are easily manageable solo. Having grown accustomed to the American way of serving cheese before the meal instead of after, I now often present a cheese board with aperitifs along with tasty nibbles, such as nuts and olives. A great tradition that features one ingredient in two different ways is the cooking and serving of duck in two parts, allowing white and dark meats to be used to their best advantage. The duck breast is the starter in this menu, quickly pan-grilled to medium-rare, sliced, and served with a salad. The main course offers the duck legs, oven-braised until the meat nearly falls off the bone, served with apples, red cabbage, and potatoes. An upside-down apple pie is the perfect finish—as would be any apple pie or tart.

TABLE AND DECORATIONS: It is said that you first enjoy a dish with your eyes, so it should be as visually appealing in its presentation as it is tasty when eaten. And a beautifully set and attractively dressed table is of equal importance, particularly on special occasions. The truly big

days, such as Christmas, Hanukkah, Thanksgiving, and Easter bring to mind certain specific elements for decorating their respective festive tables, and we bring those items out from storage at the appropriate time—along with the best china, silver, and glassware.

However, festive holiday tables can be created with equal success using a wide variety of other decorative objects of no particular holiday significance.

An avid collector of many different things, I enjoy dressing a special table with my collectibles, adding a seasonal touch to marry them to the occasion. The collection of "chicken objects" that I put on view in my first book is just part of a larger collection of all sorts of feathered and winged creatures that decorate the shelves, walls, and cupboards of our home. Almost as numerous as the chickens are the ducks. I most frequently use the former for Easter and during the spring or summer, while the latter appear on fall and winter tables. At Christmas, a wreath or other holiday greens and some fancy ribbon tie my ducks to the occasion.

Objects that are an intricate part of a room's décor year round may have their own loose ties to Christmas, needing just a single festive accent to give the room a seasonal look. In a clean modern setting, a huge basket of pine cones and a collection of deer figures, designs, and antlers provide design contrast throughout the year, but in the holiday season their associations with Christmas are seemingly the reason for their presence.

TRADITIONS: In some versions of the Christmas story, it is told that the stag was the first animal, other than those in the manger, to witness the birth of the Christ Child. And it was the stag who then raced over the hills to announce the news to the shepherds and their flocks in the fields below.

More secular in origin and certainly more commonly narrated as legend, is the reindeer's association with Santa Claus and his sleigh. It was the famous poem written by Clement Clarke Moore for his children in 1822, best known by its first line, " 'Twas the night before Christmas . . ." that seems to have introduced and popularized the idea in America that Santa's sleigh was pulled not by horses but by eight arctic deer whom he named as well. Moore's poem was soon in print all over Europe and the reindeer-pulled sleigh became part of the European Father Christmas legend too. Another purely American Christmas creation that was quickly embraced by the rest of the world is Rudolf the Red-Nosed Reindeer. The story of the ugly duckling—or reindeer—who triumphs in the end was created as a promotional piece in 1939 for the Montgomery Ward company and was written by Robert L. May. Nearly 3 million copies were sent out that year, while the story hit the 4 million mark in 1946. The words and music were brought together by Johnny Marks in 1949 for the song we all know and love today, and first recorded by cowboy singer Gene Autry.

COLLECTIBLES: *T*he oldest and most sought-after figures representing Rudolf the Red-Nosed Reindeer date from the 1950s. (Had I known, I would have kept all those plastic Rudolphs I accumulated as a child.) Representations of the original eight reindeer made famous by Moore—Dasher, Dancer, Prancer, Vixen, Comet, Cupid, Donner, and Blitzen—and other anonymous sleigh team members are prized collectibles when of a much earlier date. Most often reindeer are depicted as part of a Santa-and-sleigh vignette, particularly when they are three-dimensional objects. They do, however, sometimes appear on their own on Christmas cards and calendars.

Besides Christmas greeting and trade cards, other printed mediums are popular holiday items. Quite collectible are older examples of Advent calendars—made for the month or so leading up to December 25 with surprise messages for each of the days hidden behind paper flaps—decoratively printed almanacs, trade cards or sheets, and later calendars that local merchants offered their clientele.

Christmas stories or poems and music offer a variety of opportunities to the book, music, or specialist Christmas collector. Antique rare or special editions are unavailable to most; it is often hard to find far less special ones in excellent condition. Personally, I think every house should have a copy of the Moore classic and Dickens's *A Christmas Carol*, no matter what its dollar value, to read to the children or oneself on Christmas Eve.

The Victorian era saw the renaissance and popularization of carol singing, whose true origins can again be found in pagan rituals. The playing and singing of Christmas carols came naturally to the Victorian drawing room, where music was an important part of social life all year long. The seasonal songs reflected the values of family and church that the Victorians cherished, so handsomely bound books of traditional carols were frequently given as gifts at Christmas.

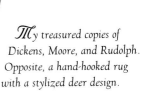

*M*y treasured copies of Dickens, Moore, and Rudolph. Opposite, a hand-hooked rug with a stylized deer design.

A casual cocktail hour is enjoyed in front of the blazing fire in the living room—the wine, cheese board, and amuse gueule (French slang for nibbles, but literally "amuse your mouth") are set out on the stone-topped coffee table in a relaxed self-service style. A collection of ornamental holiday reindeer—from Rudolph to Donner and Blitzen—are added to the year-round display of bronze, porcelain and carved wooden stags and iron deer candelabrum. The Christmas collectibles include wood, metal, composite, and plastic figures that date as early as the first part of the twentieth century.

Hors d' Oeuvres: Although we most often observe the European tradition of serving cheese at the end of the meal, I find that an interesting selection of cheeses of diverse tastes and textures to sample with wine is an easy yet distinctive beginning for special occasions. A mild and contrastingly strong goat cheese, a very aged Gouda, and a special Vacherin—a cheese so creamy you scoop it out with a spoon—are served with crackers. Trimmed celery stalks, black Moroccan olives, and French green olives along with some spiced roasted almonds make tangy taste contrasts to the cheese and will certainly "amuse."

Pan-Grilled Duck Breasts on Field Greens with Apple Cider Vinaigrette

6 to 8 ounces mâche, mixed field greens, or mesclun, washed and well drained

2 boned duck breasts (about 1 to 1¼ pounds total), skin pricked all over with a fork

1 tablespoon finely chopped thyme

Sea salt

Freshly ground black pepper

3 tablespoons Calvados or apple brandy

¼ to ⅓ cup of Apple Cider Vinaigrette (page 155)

Divide the greens among 4 serving plates.

Season the duck breasts on both sides with the thyme and salt and pepper and set aside for 20 minutes.

Slowly heat a cast-iron skillet or heavy sauté pan over medium-heat until very hot. Place the breasts in the skillet, skin side down, and cook for almost 6 minutes, until the skin is a rich golden brown. Turn the breasts over and cook for another 4 minutes for rare or 6 minutes for medium-rare. Transfer to a warm plate and loosely cover with foil.

Pour off most of the fat from the pan and return the skillet to the heat. Deglaze the pan with the Calvados, scraping up any browned bits, then pour in the vinaigrette. Heat for 1 minute, then pour the dressing into a bowl.

Cut the breasts on the diagonal into 16 slices, and arrange 4 slices on top of the greens on each plate. Whisk the dressing until thoroughly blended and spoon some over each plate. Serve immediately.

Braised Duck Legs with Apples and Red Cabbage

In front of two wood-framed nineteenth century duck prints, a ceramic platter shaped with a duck's head at one end holds candles and decorative lady apples set amongst some leaves. A terrine in the form of a duck was the packaging for some delicious pâté—with its basket-detailed bottom and duck body lid it's reminiscent of the very collectible Staffordshire "nesting hens" produced in the nineteenth century.

This dish may be prepared a day in advance and gently reheated over low heat on top of the stove. The sliced apple garnish should be prepared just before serving.

4 (12-ounce) duck legs, trimmed of excess skin and fat, skins pricked all over with the a fork, rinsed and patted dry

Vegetable oil

¼ pound salt pork, cut into 1-by-¼-inch strips

3 shallots, finely chopped (about ½ cup)

2 teaspoons chopped thyme

2 Golden Delicious apples, peeled, cored, and coarsely chopped

¼ cup plus 2 tablespoons Calvados or apple brandy

½ cup apple cider

1 cup good-quality chicken broth

1½ to 1¾ pounds red cabbage, cored, and cut into ⅜-inch slices

Sea salt

Freshly ground black pepper

2 Macoun or Empire Red apples, peeled, cored, and cut into 8 slices each, set aside in a bowl of lemon water

2 tablespoons unsalted butter

Preheat the oven to 300°F, setting the rack at the middle level.

Heat a large, heavy-bottom casserole or Dutch oven over medium-high heat until very hot. Add 2 duck legs (use a splatter screen) and brown on

(continued)

both sides, about 15 minutes total. Set aside on a plate and repeat with the other 2 legs.

Pour most of the duck fat out of the casserole (if it looks too dry, add a little oil), then add the salt pork. Cook until the strips are crisp and golden brown all over. Remove from the casserole with a slotted spoon and set aside in a small bowl. Add the shallots to the casserole and cook until translucent. Stir in the thyme and half of the chopped apples. Pour in the Calvados and bring to a boil. Stir in the cider and broth and simmer for 2 minutes.

Add half the cabbage, top with half of the browned salt pork, and stir to mix well with the apples. Place the duck legs on top, cover with the remaining cabbage, sprinkle the remaining salt pork and chopped apples over. Bring to a boil. Cover and transfer the casserole to the oven and braise for 1½ to 2 hours, until the duck is tender and easily pulls away from the bone; the cabbage should be very soft.

About 20 minutes before the duck is done, drain and pat dry the apple slices. Melt the butter in a sauté pan over medium heat and sauté the apple slices until tender and lightly golden, about 10 to 12 minutes. Set aside and keep warm.

Serve the duck legs on a bed of cabbage and garnish with apple slices.

Sautéed Potatoes

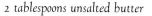

2 tablespoons unsalted butter

2 tablespoons extra-virgin olive oil

1¼ pounds Yukon Gold potatoes, peeled and chopped into ½-inch dice

Sea salt

Freshly ground black pepper

In a large nonstick skillet, melt the butter with the oil over medium-high heat, but do not let it brown. When the pan is very hot, add the potatoes and cook, tossing and stirring constantly. When the potatoes begin to brown, after 10 to 12 minutes, season with salt and pepper. Keep the potatoes moving so that they cook and brown evenly all over. Cook for about 25 minutes, until the potatoes are brown on the outside and soft in the center. Season to taste with more salt if desired.

The lattice-work patterned borders of the shallow bowl-shaped dinner plates frame images of duck, hare, and deer and would be equally as appropriate for serving a rabbit or venison stew as it is for this braised duck dish. The borders of the charger plates feature the lattice work and floral motifs alone, while the salad plates (seen on the previous page) have a large duck design in their centers.

The silver metal hunt cup (above) features a stag's head for its decorative handle. These drinking cups were worn around the necks of those riding in a traditional hunt and were used for refreshment during the spirited ride over the hills and dales of the countryside.

A 1961 calendar (below) offered by a bottling company to their clients is a die-cut print that's embossed and frosted with sparkles.

Tarte Tatin

Tarte Tatin is the upside-down apple tart that culinary legend attributes to the forgetfulness of one of the Tatin sisters, who ran a small hotel in Sologne, France, at the turn of the twentieth century. It seems that, in rushing to prepare an apple tart for dinner, she placed the properly prepared baking dish, with sugar and peeled sliced apples, in the oven, having forgotten the pastry base. Before she realized this, the tart had begun to cook and caramelize, whereupon she put the pastry on top of the apples and shoved the dish back in the oven. When the tart was done and out of the oven, she simply turned it over and out onto a plate. It was a rather fortuitous accident, as it produced one of the most tasty apple pies of all time. Béatrice Oliver's recipe here uses a method different from most versions, but leaves nothing to chance in achieving the caramelized top that makes this dessert so distinctive and delicious.

> 1 cup all-purpose flour
> ¼ cup confectioners' sugar
> ½ cup unsalted butter, at room temperature
> ½ cup granulated sugar
> 2 to 3 large tart apples, peeled, cored, and thickly sliced
> 3 tablespoons Calvados or apple brandy
> Vanilla ice cream or heavy cream

MAKE THE PASTRY: Sift the flour into a mixing bowl and cut in the butter. Using your fingertips, work the butter into the flour until the mixture is crumbly. Sift the confectioners' sugar and work it into the mixture.

Make a well in the center and add 1 teaspoon ice water. Using a fork, pull the flour mixture into the water to form a dough. If it's too crumbly and dry to form into a ball, add an additional teaspoon ice water. Form the dough into a ball, cover with plastic wrap, and refrigerate for 1 hour.

Calendars for the coming year were printed with decorative images as Christmas gifts or a form of greeting card and were made for private use or as public advertisements for businesses. Until recently, many of us have been recipients of the promotional calendar of ubiquitous design that is dropped in amongst our purchases at the liquor store or arrives in the mail from our fuel supplier. The lovely 1890 calendar (left) promotes Ivory Snow as a product that never chaps hands, and the 1926 calendar (right) from the Barker company thanks their clients and wishes them a Merry Christmas and Happy New Year. While both are trade calendars, the big bow-tied holly basket brings personal wishes of happiness from one friend to another.

MAKE THE CARAMEL: Preheat the oven to 225°F. Place a 9-inch round Pyrex dish (about 2 inches deep) on the middle rack in the oven.

Combine the granulated sugar and ½ cup water in a heavy saucepan and cook over low heat for 25 to 30 minutes; do not let it burn. When the liquid has thickened to a heavy syrup and is a rich caramel color, immediately remove the pan from the heat and the Pyrex dish from the oven. With oven mitts readily at hand, pour the caramel out into the hot dish, turning and tilting it to evenly coat the bottom and sides. Set aside.

PREPARE THE TART: Preheat the oven to 375°F, setting the rack at the middle level.

Arrange the apple slices in concentric circles in the caramel-coated Pyrex dish.

Heat the Calvados in a small saucepan until hot, then pour it over the apples and light it with a match. Set aside.

Remove the dough from the refrigerator. Lightly flour a rolling pin and work surface. Roll out the dough to a 10-inch circle about ¼-inch thick, large enough to cover the top of the apples. Place the circle of dough over the apples, folding it back over itself if it hangs down over the edges of the dish. Make a small slit in the center of the dough and place in the oven. Bake for 30 to 40 minutes, until the pastry is golden. Remove from the oven.

To turn out the tart, use a flat round plate that is slightly larger than the Pyrex dish. Wearing oven mitts, place the plate on top of the baking dish and, holding the dish and the plate, carefully turn the dish over and the tart out onto the plate. Gently lift off the baking dish. The caramelized apples will now be at the top, the pastry at the bottom. Serve while still warm with a scoop of ice cream or pass a small jug with heavy cream at the table.

To you whose friendly favors
Have helped in our success
We wish a merry Christmas
And a year of happiness
Barker & Company, Inc.

1926

Country Christmas

SERVES 8

HORS D'OEUVRES
Smoked Salmon Parcels and
Cucumber Maki Rolls

ALSACE PINOT GRIS

•

STARTER
Fresh Foie Gras and Pears

MUSCATO DI PANTELLERIA

•

MAIN COURSE
Roasted Rack of Venison

•

SIDES
Mashed Potatoes and Parsnips
Port Cranberry Sauce

POMEROL

•

DESSERT
Prune Tart

CHAMPAGNE VEUVE CLICQUOT

O little town of Bethlehem, how still we see thee lie

Nostalgic associations of Christmas with charming village settings is a prevalent holiday theme. Even as a child raised in a big city and as an adult who has until recently lived in large urban centers, I eagerly embraced the romantic notion of celebrating Christmas in an old-fashioned snow-covered village—just like the one that Currier & Ives seemed to know. Whether I am in town or country, I enjoy re-creating the feelings and the flavors of a holiday celebration set in those snowy sylvan surroundings of the good old days.

Menu: The centerpiece for this meal is venison—a hearty dish from the natural bounty of woodland forests. A rack of venison is perfect for the special holiday or festive dinner for which tradition often requires the presentation of the whole roast before it is carved and served. The two racks are presented with their rib bones crossed like an honor guard on a platter surrounded with some fresh greens and nuts—it is certain to illicit praise for the cook from those at the table. The potato and parsnip puree offers a mellow taste contrast to the tangy port cranberry sauce. Begin the evening with slices of salmon and cucumber rounds stuffed with a fish pâté—they're as good to look at as they are to eat. The fresh foie gras served with a sweet wine is a traditional treat enjoyed in France at this time of year and, accompanied by a slice of cooked pear, it is an elegant if not urbane addition to the table. As game dishes are often marinated, cooked, or served with fresh or preserved fruits, an old-fashioned prune tart is the perfect ending to the meal.

Table and Decorations: In a house designed to reproduce the style of early New England country homes, folk art, crafts, and antique furnishings are a natural backdrop to old-fashioned and rustic Christmas decorations and traditions—new or antique. The elements that make up an antique snow village, snow scenic paintings and patterned glassware, and a traditional toy Noah's Ark are the festive focal points for the downstairs rooms and table. The place settings follow the colonial American tradition of pewter and iron tableware, while complementing a collection of old iron implements displayed in the kitchen.

Ark. As a visu
tive of the Bib
was considered
suitable as a C
gift, particular
Protestant sect
miniaturized
the animals we
for instructive
it was also put
display like th
snow scenes at

Collectibl
the nineteenth
tion of acquiri
landscape wou
years. Therefor
and new togeth
looms from on
village element
have been and
shop or departm
ing the latest a
antiques shops
the early build
dle, while the
mill or a bell te
Well-made min
ers, skaters, ski
value to a colle

TRADITIO…
snow villag…
part of man…
tions have a…
tions of fig…
elements fir…
crèches or N…
evolved ov…
German Ch…
the Americ…
ally referre…
villages. W…
were restric…
gious aspec…
the later an…
figures repr…
ages paved…
opment in t…
The Germa…
nineteenth …
The arrange…
local area a…
of specific v…
but often ra…
found. The…
man settlers…
Christmas t…
Noah's Ark…

Ov…
wintry land…
ings, and ra…

The place settings for the dinner guests feature pewter plates in a style in use since Colonial times, topped with country plaid tea towels that are used as generous napkins at the holiday meal. Red snowflake printed place cards and brass jingle bells on red silk cords mark each guest's plate, while antique elves are positioned in front of each setting. A 1950s set of tall glasses printed with a charming snow village by Currier & Ives and rimmed in red are set beside green goblets to mark the colors of the season. Moravian stars are suspended from the iron chandelier. A few antique snow village buildings set in dried moss on a red tole tray make up the centerpiece, while an entire village street has been set up on an old apothecary chest behind the table and where another collection of "Santa's little helpers" are on view. A church with a steeple, a town hall, and a house or two can be lit from within with a candle. The gnomes were designed to be arranged around and under the family tree and are depicted executing a variety of elfin activities that really have nothing to do with helping Santa. The oldest pieces in the collection of houses and elves date from the 1930s and come from Germany, Japan, and America.

Smoked Salmon Parcels and Cucumber Maki

A slice of smoked salmon wrapped around a tasty filling and tied up with a strand of chive makes an attractive and delicious hors d'oeuvre—as does a thick-cut round of cucumber once its center is removed and filled with a stuffing. You can substitute your favorite fish or vegetable pâté or mousse for the filling used here.

For The Salmon

> 2 pounds presliced smoked salmon
> ⅔ cup Crab and Smoked Trout Pâté (page 24)
> 1 bunch fresh chives, washed

For The Cucumbers

> Sea salt
> 1 long European cucumber (about 16 inches)
> ¾ cup Crab and Smoked Trout Pâté (page 24)

Lay half a slice of smoked salmon (about 3-by-5 inches) on a cutting board and place 1 teaspoon of the pâté near the bottom end. Roll up the salmon from the bottom, folding in the sides as needed to keep the filling from oozing out. Tie the parcel with a long strand of chive. Place on a serving plate and repeat until all the salmon is used.

Slice the cucumber into 1-inch rounds (for about 16 pieces). Cut out the center with a small paring knife to remove the seeds and salt the opening. Set each round on some paper towels and let the pieces disgorge for about 10 minutes. Rinse the cucumbers under cold running water to remove the salt and pat dry.

Spoon the pâté into the center of the rounds, making a small mound on top. Arrange on a platter and serve with the salmon parcels.

Fresh Foie Gras and Pears

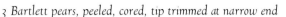

3 Bartlett pears, peeled, cored, tip trimmed at narrow end

3 tablespoons unsalted butter, broken into small bits

⅔ cup pear-infused white wine vinegar

Sea salt

Freshly ground black pepper

1 pound fresh duck foie gras, trimmed of connective tissue and veins

Preheat the oven to 350°F, setting the rack at the middle level.

Cut eight ½-inch slices from the widest part of the three pears and save the remainder for another use. Lightly grease a nonreactive baking dish with a little of the butter. Sprinkle each side of the pear slices with 2 to 3 teaspoons of the vinegar, and season with salt and pepper. Place the slices in the dish and top with the remaining butter. Cover loosely with foil. Bake for 30 to 35 minutes, until cooked through but firm. Reduce the temperature to 275°F and keep the oven door ajar for just a few minutes while the heat reduces. Keep the pear slices warm in the closed oven while cooking the foie gras.

Slicing across the lobe of the foie gras at a slight angle to cut eight ¾-inch-thick slices. Score the top side of the each slice with a crisscross design. Refrigerate until you are ready to cook them.

Heat a large nonstick skillet until very hot. Season the foie gras with salt and pepper on both sides. Slide each slice into the pan, scored side down, and cook for 2 minutes to render the fat and form a crisp brown crust. Turn and cook for 2 minutes on the other side. Transfer the foie gras to a plate, and keep warm in the oven.

Pour off two-thirds of the rendered fat and return the pan to high heat. Carefully add the remaining vinegar, whisking to scrape up any browned bits. Quickly remove the pan from the heat and pour the liquid into a small pitcher and keep warm.

Serve each slice of foie gras on top of a slice of pear, drizzle with some sauce and serve immediately.

Roasted Rack of Venison

Venison has become a very popular meat in recent years. It is frequently found on the menus of the best restaurants in America, and venison sausages and simple-to-prepare cuts can even be found in some better supermarkets. Venison's growing popularity can be attributed to the fact that it is an extremely flavorful and tender red meat that is healthful—without worrisome hormones, and low in calories, fat, and cholesterol. Today's venison doesn't require tenderizing, the marinade here simply adds flavor. For suggested sources for venison, see page 162.

In addition to the Mashed Potatoes and Parsnips, a few braised shallots would make a nice garnish. Brown 1½ pounds of peeled whole shallots in 3 tablespoons of butter, add ¼ cup of red wine, a pinch of sugar and some salt and pepper. Simmer, covered for about 40 minutes, until they are very tender, top with some butter and serve.

¼ cup Worcestershire sauce

24 juniper berries

3 cloves garlic, crushed

2 tablespoons thyme

1 tablespoon freshly cracked black peppercorns

¾ cup extra-virgin olive oil

2 racks of venison (6 to 8 ribs each), frenched and silver skin removed

Combine the Worcestershire sauce, juniper berries, garlic, thyme, peppercorns, and oil in a measuring cup and mix well.

Place the racks, ribs down, in a shallow nonreactive baking dish. Stir the marinade and pour it over the venison, turning a few times to thoroughly coat the meat. Let marinate, ribs up and the dish covered with plastic wrap, in a cool spot, for 2 hours, but not longer.

Preheat the oven to 375°F, setting the rack in the middle level.

Heat a sauté pan over medium-heat and sear each rack for about 2 minutes per

The giving of gifts at Christmas has direct connections to the exchanging of presents during the ancient Winter Solstice celebrations—like just about everything to do with this holiday—as does the consumption of ritual food or drink. Early decorated trees had ornaments that were edible or contained sweet treats to eat and were gifts hung from their branches, while an abundance of Christmas objects were made as candy containers. But the idea of offering more substantial food products presented in baskets as a thoughtful if not charitable gift is more likely a nineteenth century invention.

A basket of my cranberry sauces and some bottles of infused oils also contains a gift of Christmas hankies that can be used as cocktail napkins or to line a bread basket, and makes a handsome gift.

side. Place the racks in a roasting pan, ribs down, and insert a meat thermometer in the middle of one of the racks.

Roast for 20 minutes, or until the meat reaches an internal temperature of 120°F, or 125°F for less rare meat. Remove from the oven and transfer to a warmed serving platter, placing the 2 racks opposite each other and crossing the ribs and present to the table. Transfer the racks to a carving board, as the meat will have rested during the arranging and presentation of the dish, slice immediately into chops. Serve 1 to 2 chops or one double chop per person, depending on appetites.

Mashed Potatoes and Parsnips

2¾ pounds russet potatoes, peeled and cut into 1½-inch pieces, rinsed
1¾ pounds parsnips, peeled and cut into 1-inch pieces
2 tablespoons unsalted butter, at room temperature
Sea salt
Freshly ground white pepper
⅓ cup crème fraîche or whipping cream

Place the potatoes and parsnips in a large saucepan with enough salted water to cover them by an inch or so. Bring to a boil and cook, uncovered, for 20 to 30 minutes, until the vegetables are very tender. Drain and return the vegetables to the saucepan and place over very low heat. Add the butter and mash with a potato ricer until there are no lumps and the mixture is smooth. Season with salt and white pepper to taste. Add the crème fraîche and continue to mash until smooth and fluffy; adjust seasoning. (The dish can be made a few hours in advance, left to stand at room temperature, covered, and rewarmed over low heat before serving.) Serve hot.

A hearty dish, the choice of a roasted rack of venison is particularly fitting for a country style Christmas. Presenting the venison to the guests at the table before it is carved—the roasted meat set on a platter surrounded with some fresh leaves and nut-bearing branches, the two racks with their rib bones crossed like an honor guard— follows the tradition of the host presenting the roasted holiday bird. Rich game meats like venison are often prepared or served with fortified wines or preserved fruits, while juniper berries and bay leaves are a constant feature in their dishes. Root vegetables or dark leafy greens make perfect side dishes as their flavors stand up to the taste of the meat. Along with the potato and parsnip purée, a dish of braised whole shallots or Swiss chard could be served. Cook the shallots according to the instructions in the headnote on page 148, and use the recipe for Wilted Swiss Chard on page 121. The tangy Port Cranberry Sauce is the perfect taste contrast to the venison (see page 156).

Prune Tart

———— ✦ ————

*Y*ou'll need to soak the prunes overnight for this recipe.

Unsalted butter

Flour for dusting

½ recipe Sweet Short Crust Pastry Dough (page 158), chilled

1 pound dried beans for blind baking

28 to 30 dried pitted prunes, soaked overnight in a mixture of ¼ cup Armagnac
   and ¼ cup strong tea

3 eggs

½ cup plus 1 tablespoon heavy cream

⅓ cup plus 1 tablespoon whole milk

2 tablespoons confectioners' sugar

Preheat oven to 375°F, setting the rack at the middle level.

Grease and lightly flour the inside of a 10-inch fluted loose-bottom tart pan.

Cut the chilled dough ball into ¼-inch slices, placing the slices in the tart pan
one at a time and pressing down on them to mold to the shape of the tin, covering the
bottom and sides evenly. Prick the surface of the dough all over with a fork. Place a
piece of parchment paper over the entire surface of the dough in the tin, and fill with
dried beans. Bake for 30 minutes.

Remove from the oven, take out the paper and beans, and set aside to cool before
proceeding.

Reserving one whole prune, cut the remaining prunes in half. Arrange the sliced
halves on the pastry crust in concentric circles, their tops pointing into the center.

Combine the eggs, cream, milk, and sugar in a mixing bowl. Using a wire whisk
or an electric hand mixer, beat until the mixture is frothy. Pour the egg mixture over
the prunes and bake for about 45 minutes, until the crust is golden and the sides have
come away from the edges of the pan. Remove from the oven and let cool. Push up the
base of the pan and remove the tart to a serving plate. The tart is best served warm.

*I*ron and metal objects hold old-fashioned
Christmas candies and modern favorites
wrapped for the season. The star-topped tree
made of metal bands folds up for storage and
traditionally was used to display Christmas
cards, but here is decorated with holiday
ornaments, lacquered silhouettes in a folk
style from Sweden. The tree decorated with
individual pieces of candy originally would
have held tiny candles.

THE PANTRY

This section contains some basic recipes needed for the menus contained in the book.

Basic Vinaigrette

¼ teaspoon sea salt

8 grindings black pepper

1 tablespoon Dijon mustard

2 teaspoons minced shallot

¼ cup white wine vinegar

⅓ cup extra-virgin olive oil

¼ cup peanut oil

Combine the salt, pepper, mustard, shallots, and vinegar in a measuring cup or bowl. Mix the two oils together in another measuring cup and gradually whisk them into the vinegar mixture, pouring in a slow steady stream.

MAKES ¾ CUP (8 TO 10 SERVINGS)

Variations

For Cilantro Vinaigrette (used in the recipe on page 33), follow the Basic Vinaigrette recipe and add 1 tablespoon finely chopped fresh cilantro at the end.

For Tarragon Vinaigrette (used in the recipe on page 46), follow the Basic Vinaigrette recipe and stir in 1 table-spoon finely chopped fresh tarragon leaves at the end. You may also substitute a tarragon-flavored vinegar for the white wine vinegar.

For Apple Cider Vinaigrette (used in the recipe on page 132), follow the Basic Vinaigrette recipe and add 2 teaspoons applesauce, and substitute apple cider–flavored vinegar for the white wine vinegar.

CRANBERRY SAUCES

....

Each of the sauces has been paired with specific dishes in the menus, but some work equally well with other dishes in this book and all are good complements to game, pork, or poultry throughout the year. These sauces can be prepared up to 1 week in advance. Bring to room temperature before serving.

Maple-Walnut Cranberry Sauce

Recommended to accompany Fresh Ham with Maple-Walnut Cranberry Glaze on page 26.

¾ cup cranberry juice

½ cup pure maple syrup

¼ teaspoon maple extract

¼ cup brown sugar

12 ounces fresh cranberries

Combine the cranberry juice, syrup, maple extract, and brown sugar in a saucepan over medium heat and simmer for 5 minutes. Add the cranberries and bring to a boil. Reduce the heat and simmer for about 10 minutes, until the cranberries have popped and the mix-ture is a bit thick and syrupy. Remove from the heat and let cool. Transfer to an attractive glass jar or other container and refrigerate for at least 1 day.

Pear-Ginger Cranberry Sauce

Recommended to accompany Turkey Breast Stuffed with Apples, Cinnamon, and Thyme on page 28.

¼ cup cranberry juice

2 tablespoons orange juice

1 cup sugar

1 tablespoon plus 1 teaspoon grated fresh ginger

1 cup chopped, peeled, and cored ripe pears (1 to 2 pears)

12 ounces fresh cranberries

(continued)

Combine the juices, sugar, and ginger in a saucepan over medium heat and simmer for 2 minutes, or until the sugar has dissolved. Add the pears and cranberries and bring to a boil. Reduce the heat and simmer for 10 to 15 minutes, until the pears are tender and the cranberries have popped. Remove from the heat and let cool. Transfer to an attractive glass jar or other container and refrigerate for at least 1 day.

Port Cranberry Sauce

Recommended to accompany Rack of Venison on page 148.

1 cup Ruby port
¾ cup dark brown sugar
6 juniper berries
5 thin orange slices, halved
1 (3-inch) stick cinnamon
Pinch of sea salt
12 ounces fresh cranberries

Combine the port, brown sugar, juniper berries, orange slices, cinnamon stick, and salt in a saucepan over medium heat and simmer for 15 minutes. Remove and discard the juniper berries, orange slices, and the cinnamon and add the cranberries. Bring to a boil, then reduce the heat and simmer for 10 to 15 minutes, until the cranberries have popped and the liquid is thick and syrupy. Remove from the heat and let cool. Transfer to an attractive glass jar or other container and refrigerate for at least 1 day.

Spicy Cranberry Sauce

Recommended to accompany Deep-Fried Turkey on page 64.

¼ cup cranberry juice
⅜ cup honey
½ tablespoon grated orange zest
½ stick cinnamon
1 small bay leaf
½ teaspoon grated fresh ginger
¼ teaspoon ground coriander
¼ teaspoon kosher or coarse salt
¼ teaspoon freshly ground black pepper
Pinch or two of cayenne pepper
6 ounces fresh cranberries
2 orange sections, peeled

Combine the cranberry juice, honey, and orange zest in a saucepan over medium heat and bring to a simmer; cook for 5 minutes. Add the cinnamon stick, bay leaf, ginger, coriander, salt, pepper, and cayenne and simmer for 5 minutes.

Add the cranberries and continue to simmer, stirring occasionally until the berries have popped and the sauce is thick. Remove from the heat, add the orange sections and let sit for several minutes. Once cool, transfer to an attractive glass jar or other container and refrigerate for at least 1 day. Remove cinnamon stick and bay leaf before serving.

VEGETABLES
....

Asparagus

Recommended to accompany the Roasted Salmon on page 48, and for the filling of the Vol-au-Vents on page 119.

Sea salt
1 pound thin asparagus, woody part trimmed, washed

In a low wide saucepan or sauté pan wide enough to hold the asparagus lying down flat in a few layers, bring salted water to a boil. Add the asparagus, return to a boil, and cook for 3 to 4 minutes, until their stems are tender. Remove the pan from the heat. Using kitchen tongs, quickly transfer the asparagus to drain on paper towels. If serving cold or using later, chill under cold running water and drain.

Cauliflower

Prepare for the Grape Tomato, Broccoli, and Cauliflower Salad on page 33.

Sea salt
3 heads of cauliflower, trimmed and cut florets into bite-sized pieces

Bring a large saucepan of salted water to a boil. Add the cauliflower florets and bring back to a boil. Boil for 2 to 3 minutes, until just tender. Drain. If serving cold or using later, chill under cold running water and drain.

Broccoli

Prepare this way for the Grape Tomato, Broccoli, and Cauliflower Salad on page 33.

> *Sea salt*
> *2½ pounds broccoli crowns, trimmed and cut into bite-sized florets*

Bring a large saucepan of salted water o a boil. Add the broccoli florets and bring back to a boil. Boil for 3 to 5 minutes, until just tender. Drain. If serving cold or using later, chill under cold running water and drain.

Haricots Verts

Recommended to accompany the Pheasant on page 102.

> *2 pounds haricots verts, rinsed and tips trimmed*
> *Sea salt*
> *Freshly ground black pepper*

Bring a large saucepan of water to a boil. add the green beans and bring back to a boil. Cook for 3 to 4 minutes, until they are just tender. (Cook longer if you prefer them with less crunch.) Remove the pan from the heat and drain. Season with salt and pepper.

Slow-Cooked Leeks

Recommended to accompany Roasted Salmon on page 48.

> *20 thin or 10 thick leeks, trimmed to include some green, washed, sliced into ¼-inch rounds, then soaked and thoroughly drained*
> *Sea salt*
> *2 to 3 tablespoons finely chopped chives or parsley (optional)*
> *Freshly ground black pepper*

Slowly heat a nonstick sauté pan over very low heat. Add 2 tablespoons water, the leeks, and a pinch of salt. Cover and cook gently over the lowest heat for 45 to 50 minutes, until the leeks are very soft. It is important to maintain a low heat and slow cooking, so check on the leeks from time to time—ideally, a clear lid should be used.

When the leeks are done, stir in the chives if desired, and season with pepper and more salt to taste.

Polenta Loaf

Used in recipe for Polenta Toasts on page 105.

> *Sea salt*
> *2 cups instant polenta (quick-cooking)*

Bring 6 cups water and 1 teaspoon salt to a boil in a large deep saucepan. Stirring, gradually pour in the polenta. Reduce the heat to a simmer and cook for 4 to 6 minutes, until the mixture is very thick and the water has been absorbed.

Spoon the polenta into a 9-by-5-by-3-inch loaf pan and let it stand for about 10 to 20 minutes, until it has set and is firm, like a cake. Turn the polenta onto a plate.

(Wrapped in a tea towel and refrigerated, the loaf can keep for a few days.)

Wild Rice

Used in recipe for Wild Rice and Risotto Jambalaya Dressing on page 68, it can be made a few hours in advance and brought to room temperature before making the Jambalaya.

> *Sea salt*
> *½ cup wild rice, rinsed well and drained*

Put 2 cups water and ⅛ teaspoon salt in a saucepan and add the wild rice. Bring to a full boil, cook for 1 minute, then reduce the heat, cover, and simmer over low heat. Cook for 45 to 60 minutes, until all the water has been absorbed and the rice has burst open.

Transfer to a bowl.

Himalayan Red Rice

Used in recipe for Wild Rice and Risotto Jambalaya Dressing on page 68, it can be made a few hours in advance and brought to room temperature before making the Jambalaya.

(continued)

Sea salt

½ cup Himalayan red rice, rinsed well and drained

Put 1½ cups water and ⅛ teaspoon salt in a saucepan and add the wild rice. Bring to a full boil, cook for 1 minute, then reduce the heat, cover, and simmer over low heat. Cook for 20 to 40 minutes, until all the water has been absorbed and the rice has puffed up but is still firm. Transfer to a bowl.

Basic Risotto

Used in recipe for Wild Rice and Risotto Jambalaya Dressing on page 68, it can be made a few hours in advance and brought to room temperature before making the Jambalaya.

3 tablespoons unsalted butter

½ onion, finely chopped

1 cup Arborio (short-grained) rice

⅓ cup dry white wine

3 to 4 cups chicken broth, warmed

Heat the butter in a saucepan over medium heat. Add the onion and cook until translucent and soft, 5 minutes. Add the Arborio rice and cook, stirring, until a white dot appears at the center of the rice grains, about 2 minutes. Pour in the wine and cook, stirring until the liquid is absorbed.

Ladle ¾ cup of the warm broth and cook, stirring until the liquid is absorbed. Keep adding the broth, ¼ cup at a time, stirring, until the rice has puffed up and has a thick, creamy consistency, and all the liquid has been absorbed (you may not use up all the broth). The rice should be a bit firm to the bite. Transfer to a bowl.

PASTRY DOUGH

....

Puff Pastry Dough

Used in recipes for the Vol-au-Vents on page 119 and Gateaux des Roi, page 122.

3 cups all-purpose flour

2 teaspoons sea salt

4 sticks unsalted butter, 1 stick cut into small dice

¾ cup plus 2 tablespoons ice water

Sift the flour and the salt into a large mixing bowl. Add the diced butter and rub the flour and the butter together with your fingers to make a crumbly mixture. Make a well in the center and pour in ¾ cup plus 2 tablespoons ice water, and use a fork to incorporate it into the flour mixture until a smooth dough forms.

Lightly flour a work surface. Place the dough on the work surface and form it into a ball. Lightly flour the dough ball, wrap it tightly in plastic wrap, and refrigerate for 30 minutes.

Put the remaining 3 sticks of butter between two sheets of parchment paper. With a lightly floured rolling pin, roll out the butter to a thickness of about a half an inch, and trim it to a 6-inch square. Refrigerate for 20 minutes or so.

Remove the dough and butter from the refrigerator. Place the dough on a lightly floured work surface and roll out to a 12-inch square. Remove the butter from the paper and place it in the center of the square of dough, setting it on a diagonal. Fold the corners of the dough over the butter so they meet in the center. Lightly flour the rolling pin and roll out the dough to a 12-by-8-inch rectangle.

Fold the rectangle into thirds, and turn it 90 degrees. Roll it out again into a 12-by-8-inch rectangle.

Wrap the dough in plastic wrap and refrigerate for 30 minutes.

Repeat this process exactly, rolling, turning, and refrigerating, 2 more times. After a total of 3 turns, 6 rollings, and 90 minutes of refrigeration, the dough is ready to use. (The dough can be refrigerated for up to 4 days or kept frozen, well wrapped, for up to a few months.)

Sweet Short Crust Pastry Dough

Used in recipe for Prune Tart, page 152.

2⅓ cups all purpose flour, sifted

3 stick unsalted butter, softened, cut into small bites

⅔ cup plus 3 tablespoons confectioners' sugar

3 large egg yolks

Combine the flour and butter in the bowl of a food processor and pulse until the mixture resembles fine bread crumbs. Add the sugar and pulse to combine, then add the egg yolks, one at a time, and process, stopping to scrape down the sides of the bowl when necessary.

Process until the mixture comes together into a ball.

Remove the dough from the bowl, wrap tightly in plastic wrap, and refrigerate for 1 hour before using. (The dough can be refrigerated for up to 4 days or kept frozen, well wrapped, for up to a few months.) Makes enough dough for 2 single 10-inch crusts.

Short Crust Pastry Dough

Used in recipe for Tartlets, page 22.

2 cups all-purpose flour, sifted
1 stick plus 2 tablespoons unsalted butter at room temperature, cut into small bits

Combine the flour and butter in a bowl and blend together to a crumbly consistency (there should be no big lumps). Add ⅔ cup of ice water and stir with a fork until the mixture comes together into a ball. Remove the dough from the bowl, wrap tightly in plastic wrap, for about 10 minutes before using. (The dough can be refrigerated for up to 4 days and kept frozen, well wrapped, for up to a few months.) Makes enough for 2 single 10-inch pie crusts or 40 2¼-inch tartlets.

Coconut Shortbread Cookies

2 sticks unsalted butter
2 tablespoons grated dessicated unsweetened coconut
3 teaspoons unsweetened coconut milk
⅔ cup confectioner's sugar, sifted
2 cups all purpose flour, sifted
½ teaspoon salt

Cream the butter in a food processor. Add the coconut and coconut milk and blend well. Pour in the sugar, flour, and salt and process until the dough forms.

Remove the dough from the mixer, place on a lightly floured surface, knead a few times and make into a round ball.

With a lightly floured rolling pin, roll out the dough to a ¼ inch thickness.

Using a variety of cookie cutters in Christmas design shapes, cut out the cookies. Prick the surface of the cookies with a fork about 4 times, and create an attractive decorative pattern on them.

Place the cookie shapes onto a baking sheet covered with greaseproof paper and refrigerate for 10 minutes.

While the first batch of cookies are chilling, gather up the dough remainders, form into a ball, roll out to ¼ inch thickness and cut out more cookies.

Repeat process as with the first batch of cookies.

When all the dough has been used, and all the cookies chilled for 10 minutes, place the tray in the oven and bake for 20 minutes.

Macaroni and Cheese

Recommended as the starter course for the children in the Christmas Day Lunch menu on page 55.

Sea salt
¼ pound elbow macaroni
2 tablespoons unsalted butter
1 cup evaporated milk
Mild dry mustard powder
1 large egg, lightly beaten
1½ cups processed American cheese, cut into small pieces
Freshly ground black pepper (optional)

Bring 1¼ quarts water to a boil, add a pinch of salt, drizzle in a touch of oil, and add the macaroni, stirring. Cook until almost tender.

While the macaroni is cooking, gently warm a Dutch oven over very low heat. When the macaroni is done, drain, then add the macaroni to the Dutch Oven, and stir in the butter. Remove from the heat and set aside.

Warm the evaporated milk and add a pinch of the mustard powder, then combine with the egg, cheese, and a pinch of salt and pepper in a bowl and stir until well mixed.

Return the Dutch oven to a low heat and gradually stir in the cheese mixture. Cook for 5 to 6 minutes, until the cheese sauce has thickened, is creamy, and heated through.

APPENDIX

Bibliography

Bartlett, John and Kaplan, Justin
Bartlett's Familiar Quotations
16th edition, Little, Brown &
Company, Boston, 1992

Chalmers, Irena
The Great American Christmas Almanac,
Viking Studio Books,
Viking Penguin Inc., New York, 1988

Grant, George and Wilbur, Gregory
Christmas Spirit, Cumberland House,
Nashville Tennessee, 1999

Johnson, George
*Christmas, Ornaments, Lights and
Decorations: Collector's Identification
and Value Guide, Volumes I, II and III,*
Collector Books, a Division of Schroeder
Publishing Company, Kentucky, 1987
and 1997

King, Constance
*Christmas, Antiques, Decorations and
Traditions,* Antique Collectors' Club
Limited, Suffolk, England, 1999

Parents Magazine
Christmas Holiday Book, Parents'
Magazine Press, New York, 1972

The Glory and Pageantry of Christmas,
Time-Life Books, New Jersey, 1963

Schiffer, Margaret
Christmas Ornaments: A Festive Study,
Schiffer Publishing Co., Pennsylvania,
1995

Snyder, Jeffrey B. and Stoltzfirs, Dawn
*White Ironstone: A Survey of Its Many
Forms,* Schiffer Publishing Co.,
Pennsylvania, 1997

Snyder, Jeffrey B.
*Historical Staffordshire: American Patriouts
and Views,* Schiffer Publishing Co.,
Pennsylvania, 1995

Snyder, Phillip
December 25th: The Joys of Christmas,
Dodd Mead & Company, New York,
1985

Snyder, Phillip, Roy Coggin
*The History of the Christmas Tree and
Antique Christmas Ornaments,*
Penguin, New York, 1990

Stevens, Patricia
Merry Christmas: A History of the Holiday,
MacMillan Publishing Company,
New York, 1979

Von Drachenfels, Suzanne
The Art of the Table,
Simon & Schuster, New York, 2000

Vaughn, Mary Ann Woloch
Ukrainian Christmas,
Ukrainian Heritage Company, 1983

Sources

The following shops and manufacturers generously loaned merchandise for use in this book.

ANTIQUES AND COLLECTIBLES

Olde Antiques Market
The Green House at
Jenifer House Commons
Rt. 7 Stockbridge Road
Great Barrington, MA 01230
tel 413-528-1840
fax 413-528-4730
pages 46, 54, 77, 86, 104, 105, 120, 121, 134, 146

Coffman's Antiques Markets
Jenifer House Commons
RT. 7 Stockbridge Road
P.O. Box 592
Great Barrington, MA 01230
tel 413-528-9282 & 528-9602
www.antiquejunction.com/coffmans
email ccamjc@vgernet.net
page 131

The Everlastings Shop
1701 Route 9D
Cold Spring, NY 10516

CONTEMPORARY FOLK ARTS AND CRAFTS

The Birdhouse Gallery
280 Main Street
Great Barrington, MA 01230
tel 413-528-0984
www.birdhousegallery.com
page 102

Homescapes
149 Main Street
Cooperstown, NY 13326
tel 607-547-8425
page 100

McAdoo Rugs
1 Pleasant Street
North Bennington, VT 05257
tel 802-442-3563
www.mcadoorugs.com
pages 103, 128

CHRISTMAS DECORATIONS

Kurt S. Adler-Santa's World
1107 Broadway,
New York, NY 10010
tel 800-243-XMAS (9627)
pages 20, 21, 30, 32, 38, 97, 108, 109, 111, 113, 122

ACCESSORIES FOR THE HOME AND TABLE

April 56
336 Main Street
Lakeville, CT 06039
tel 860-435-2623
pages 75, 96–99, 134

Gracious Home
1217 Third Avenue
New York, NY 10021
tel 212-988-8990
pages 102, 141, 168

KITCHENWARES

The Different Drummer
374 Pittsfield Road
Lenox, MA 01240
tel 800-375-COOK (2665)
e-mail ddrummer@taconic.net
page 127

The following are some recommended food product brands.

MEAT, GAME AND POULTRY, PÂTÉS, SAUSAGES:

D'Artangnan
280 Wilson Avenue
Newark, NJ 07015
tel 800 DARTAGNAN
www.dartagnan.com

Plainville Farms
7830 Plainville Road
Plainville, NY 13137
tel 800-724-0206
www.plainvillefarms.com

Murray's
334 Main Street
So. Fallsburg, NY 12779
tel 800-770-6347
www.murrayschicken.com

Les Trois Cochons
453 Greenwich Street
New York, NY 10013
tel 800-Les-Pates (537-7283)
www.3pigs.com
(and vegetable terrines)

COOKING BROTH

Imagine
1245 San Carlos Avenue
San Carlos, CA 94070
tel 650-595-6300
www.imaginefoods.com

Shelton's Poultry Inc.
204 N. Lorraine
Pomona, CA 91767
tel 800-541-1833
www.sheltons.com

RICES

Lotus Foods Inc.
921 Richmond Street
El Cerrito, CA 94530
tel 510-525-3137
www.worldofrice.com

Lundberg Family Farms
5370 Church Street
PO Box 369
Richvale, CA 55974-0369
tel 530-882-4551
www.lundberg.com

CHEESE

Murray's Cheese Shop
257 Bleecker Street
New York, NY 10014
tel 888-692-4339
www.murrayscheese.com

Ideal Cheese
942 First Avenue
New York, NY 10022
tel 800-382-0109
www.idealcheese.com

John Wm. Macy's Cheesesticks
80 Kipp Avenue
Elmwood Park, NJ 07407
tel 800-643-0573
www.cheesesticks.com

Polder Thermo-Timer
8 Slater Street
Port Chester, NY 10573
tel 800-431-2133
www.polder.com

INDEX

(Page numbers in *italic* refer to illustrations.)

. . . and to all a good night.